WINNING
NOW

WINNING NOW

A Playbook for Good Government

Raul Torres, CPA

AuthorHouse™ LLC
1663 Liberty Drive
Bloomington, IN 47403
www.authorhouse.com
Phone: 1-800-839-8640

Permissions
Raul Torres, CPA
4118 Ayers St., Corpus Christi, TX 78415
Or email raul@raultorrescpa.com

Published by AuthorHouse 02/28/2014

ISBN: 978-1-4918-6902-4 (sc)
ISBN: 978-1-4918-6903-1 (e)

Library of Congress Control Number: 2014904111

This book is dedicated to my mother, my step dad, my family, and all my friends, volunteers, and supporters that made our many campaigns for public office possible.

We dreamed, we worked and waged a good fight.
We did well. We did the impossible.
We did not labor in vain for in our quest of
Perfection we achieved Excellence.
And our dreams remain alive within each one of us.

May God bless all of you and may God always bless America.

Contents

Introduction

"Winning is not a sometime thing; it's an all-time thing. You don't win once in a while, you don't do things right once in a while, you do them right all the time. Winning is habit."—*Vince Lombardi*

Vince Lombardi knows a thing or two about winning. Coach Lombardi is the standard by which all other football coaches are measured because he was the most successful football coach of his time. The keys to Coach Lombardi's success can be summarized in these simple, but powerful principles: commitment, truth, excellence, passion, mental toughness, and discipline. These simple, powerful principles created the greatest football dynasty in history. Individually, the Green Bay Packers were just regular football players, but as a team, they were World Champions.

How great where they? The Packers had nine straight winning seasons that resulted in five NFL World Championships and they were the winners of the first two Super Bowl games. Coach Lombardi proved that when people of come together with a common purpose and they commit themselves to pursue perfection then they could achieve excellence.

This is what this book, *Winning Now*, is all about. It's about empowering average citizens to achieve excellence in their government. If you are willing to dedicate yourself to commitment, truth, passion, mental toughness, and discipline then you can achieve what most people say is impossible to do, change your government. I invite you to take this journey with me and by working together I believe we can restore America to what Almighty God intended her to be "that shining city on a hill."

The Fight For Freedom

Our journey begins in the year 1863. That was the year President Abraham Lincoln issued the Emancipation of Proclamation. Though many slaves had been declared free by Lincoln's 1863 Emancipation of Proclamation, their post-war status was uncertain. Then on April 8, 1864, the Senate passed the 13th Amendment to abolish slavery. The House followed suit on January 31, 1865 and the states quickly followed suit to ratify the amendment. Finally, on December 6, 1865 the 13th Amendment to the United States Constitution become law.

The measure abolished slavery and involuntary servitude, except as punishment for a crime, yet it took America another 100 years to fully implement the intent of our Founding Fathers when they wrote in the Declaration of Independence that all men are created equal by God.

The Civil Rights Movement of the 1960's featured the courage of Martin Luther King. Mr. King sought justice and equality among all Americans. His words ignited a passion among the American people resulting in millions of Americans who joined him in taking this message of equality to the streets and finally to the halls of Congress. His crusade to finally bring true equality to all American citizens was achieved when Congress and President Lyndon Johnson passed into law the Civil Rights Act of 1964. This law embodied the vision of our Founding Fathers and President Lincoln who saw an America as the land of opportunity whereby men could be free to live, prosper, and pursue their happiness for themselves and their families just as God had intended since the beginning.

Now almost 50 years later the issue of freedom in America is once again one of the dominant issues of the day among hardworking Americans. This freedom is different than what has confronted America in her past. This freedom is an attack upon all Americans. The issue of today is what role government should play in our lives, in our schools, and in our lives. The idea that government has gotten too big and therefore a threat to its citizens is of great concern to many Americans. This state of concern is real.

The forces that have infiltrated many of government's highest elected offices are taking action that clearly reveals they desire to take American down a path that leads toward a society based on the principles of Socialism. For millions of God fearing, patriotic Americans they now believe that our nation's founding principles and our individual freedoms are now under attack. Looking back through history we quickly learn that the fight for freedom never ends if man desires to remain free.

"Freedom is never more than one generation away from extinction. We didn't pass it to our children in the bloodstream. It must be fought for, protected, and handed on for them to do the same."—Ronald Reagan

The Tea Party Gets Involved

The issue of freedom was and continues to be the driving force behind the uprising of what has become called "the Tea Party movement." It can be traced to February 19, 2009 when CNBC's Rick Santelli, while standing on the Chicago Mercantile Exchange floor, vocally condemned the Obama Administration's proposal to help homeowners facing foreclosure refinance their mortgages. This action is credited with launching the grassroots movement.[1]

The Tea Party's involvement in the 2010 elections resulted in the election of a large number of new freshmen U.S. Representatives in Washington D.C. and perhaps the biggest win came in the state of Kentucky where Tea Party candidate, Rand Paul, despite the fact that he had never previously held political office, defeated Kentucky Attorney General Jack Conway to become one of the state's two U.S. Senators.[1]

In addition, many local and statewide tea party supported candidates either won their respective races or were very competitive and set the stage for them to return for resurgence in the 2012 General Elections where they managed to win some big races in states all over America. Perhaps the biggest victory by a Tea Party supported candidate was the race won by the virtually unknown, Ted Cruz who defeated Lt. Governor David Dewhurst for the U.S. Senate in the Republican Primary race for the state of Texas. Mr. Cruz went on to handily win against his Democrat opponent in the General Election that was held in November.

Not since the Civil Right marches of the 1960's has the American public taken to the streets to protest the work of the American political leaders. The impact of the Tea Party cannot be measured in dollar signs or some quantitative measurement, but they definitely had an impact. They didn't win very many races, but they managed to capture the minds of millions of average hard working American citizens all across America. With the onset of the Tea Party movement Americans everywhere seem to now be taking a personal interest in what their government was doing domestically and internationally.

Today, Americans are concerned not only for their future, but of the continued existence of the traditional American way of life we have had since the founding of America. Due to the various scandals arising out of the Obama Administration over the past two years such as Fast and Furious, Benghazi, IRS, and the NSA listening in to millions of American cell and phone calls it seems that the American public is now more engaged in listening, watching, interacting on social sites, and talking with their elected officials more than ever in our nation's history. This is truly something good for America.

I believe God had a divine purpose when he created this great land we call America. God created a special place for those who had a special love of freedom and the courage to leave the homeland only to face unknown dangers just for the opportunity to be free men.

From our forefathers to our modern-day immigrants, we've come from every corner of the earth only to be called Americans. Since that time, we are surrounded by a great cloud of witnesses, our forefathers, whose lives and stories serve as a reminder of the true cost of freedom. All over the world man's desire to experience freedom and to live free has not dimmed, but rather we see it every day all around us.

On any given day, you will see people from all walks of life busy at work, getting an education, or starting a new business all in the hopes that one day their dreams will come true and they do it all despite the interferences and hardships placed upon them by the federal government.

Therefore, now more than ever, people from are being more active in the political process and are taking a closer look at the work of their local, state, and federal government and of their elected leaders. They are asking more questions about government than ever before and they are demanding more answers.

America is a land filled with the most freedom loving, charitable people in the whole world, yet we are also a nation plagued with problems. People today are demanding solutions, not legislative action that kicks the can down the road so it becomes somebody else's problem. They want real solutions with measurable results. Americans are tired of cute television commercials and more political doubletalk. They are tired of all the political spin and mudslinging. They want the truth even if it hurts, at least then we know what we are facing. But, I am afraid that these changes will never take place until you and I demand them from our leaders at the federal, state and local levels. Washington D.C. is broken, Austin is mired in bureaucracy and traditions, and most City Halls all over America lack true leadership because the answer to all their problems is typically the need to raise more taxes.

Most of our elected leaders are totally disconnected from the reality of everyday life. The bubble they have created for themselves shields them from the needs of everyday citizens. They have created for themselves a whole new universe where laws and policies they pass do not apply to them, but rather they have special laws and privileges that no one else has.

Today, one could argue that our current form of elected leaders resemble the same form of tyrannical government, composed of royal families, nobles, lords, and the privileged, that led to America war on independence from Great Britain. In addition, there are many states such as Illinois and California that mirror their federal counterparts. You know what I am talking about. It's when a few elite people run government and others must follow their command or else be crushed and defeated so that their voices are not heard.

My friends, this should not be happening in America. Our country is headed in the wrong direction and we know it. But it seems that many people are in denial because the thought of such a reality is too terrible to accept. The fact is that our country is losing those values that made America the "shining city on the hill," the greatest country God has ever established in human history. Her days are numbered unless you and I stand and fight and defend our freedoms now.

Winning Now is a book for anyone who wants to know how to transform their local, city, state or federal government from being ordinary to achieving excellence as I refer to as "good government." In order to do this we must first understand the political and legislative process. I believe it is time we demand more from our government and those who are in charge of government. Most of our leaders will not to tell you the truth because if they did, there would be a rebellion on Election Day all across America. The fact of the matter is that their failed leadership has gotten us in the financial mess we are in at all levels of government. If they try to tell you that is not so, don't you believe them for a minute.

This is a "how to" book. The ideas in this book provide proven, common sense solutions to some of our most difficult challenges regardless of whether we are talking about local, state, or federal government. The ideas shared in this book are proven to work, yet they are not popular among our elected leaders.

Time after time I have attended a forum, conference, or meeting hosted by some elected official only to hear them and their invited guest speakers talk about how great things are under their leadership. They talk and talk, they promise and promise and they will look at you with a straight face and tell they have a plan to fix the many problems we are facing. The truth is they seldom ever do, blaming others for their failures. John Adams once said, *"Facts are stubborn things"* and I completely agree they most certainly are. The fact is elected officials should be held accountable for the promises they made during their campaign and failed to keep.

If you are like me, fed up with our ineffective elected representatives, then I encourage you to use the ideas in this book to demand action and get more attention from your elected leaders. If they refuse to listen, then fire them and let's find new leadership that will get the job done.

This book can be used as your roadmap for more efficient and more effective government. I will share with you some ideas you can use to get your elected leaders to work for you, listen to you, and more importantly deliver measurable results on issues that matter most to you and your community. Even though most of the material written in this book is focused on transforming your state government, the ideas and principles presented here will work for any level of government.

About 30 years ago, President Ronald Reagan said something that I believe is applicable to our current state of affairs. He said, *"There are no easy answers, but there are simple answers. We must have the courage to do what we know is morally right."* So there you have it my friend. What remains to be answered is, "Do you have the kind of elected leader that can provide you with simple answers and who is willing to do what is morally right" If you do, consider yourself blessed, to have someone who understands and is willing to work with you to get things done correctly. However, if you don't then the rest of this book is for you.

Raul Torres, CPA

I invite you to join me as we begin the journey to transform your state government. Our goal is to pursue perfection in all that government does for us and in that process achieve excellence in how our government serves "We the People". We begin with a look at the number one problem we have in our government.

"Freedom is never voluntarily given by the oppressor; it must be demanded by the oppressed."—Martin Luther King, Jr.

Our Government Is Broken

"My reading of history convinces me that most bad government has grown out of too much government."—John Sharp Williams

The Problem

Taking a closer look at politics in Texas I am sadden to have to say, *"Government is broken."* As a member of the Appropriations Committee in 2011, I saw firsthand how our state government spent money on things it shouldn't and failed to spend money on things it should. It's clear to see that our different levels of government takes no responsibility for the future, and it has, over the years, taken action that has suffocated many of our daily freedoms under an ever growing blanket of unnecessary bureaucracy, regulations, taxation, and growth of government even right here in "conservative" Texas.

Looking at this issue with an open mind I believe that both the Democratic and Republican parties are to blame. Appealing to our better nature, many of our elected politicians promise us short-term fixes to our most important problems. They give us noble, but vain promises that in the near future they are going to reduce the growth of entitlements and reduce our overall tax burden. Yet, this seldom occurs. The truth is that all this is just ear pleasing political double talk designed to keep us somewhat quiet and present them as being on our side.

Another thing that I noticed and seen is how many career politicians in Austin have learned, like their Washington cohorts, how to give away hundreds of millions of our tax dollars to their corporate buddies all under the cover of "economic development." This often results in big dollar political campaign contributions and lavish dinners and parties.

In exchange, they have learned to give us those non-monetary political victories such as legislative victories on social issues. When it comes to adopting sound conservative fiscal policy legislation those pieces of legislation never even get out of committee much less on the floor for a vote. In other words, when it comes to conservative based fiscal policies the Austin politicians allow them to never see the light of day.

Some Are Noble Servants

Not all elected politicians fall under the category above. Many are true patriots and desire what is best for the country rather than what is best for their political careers. However, these kinds of men and women are quietly kept under control either through lame duck committee assignments or the killing of their legislation in committee.

Truly the latest performance coming out of Austin and Washington has not been our nation's finest hour. Instead, it has been an embarrassment to all Americans. The American people deserve more from their representatives in Washington and the people of Texas deserve a lot more from their representatives in Austin.

Don't Be Surprised

This has been going on for the past 10 years in Texas government all under the disguise of "conservative leadership." The result has been bigger and bigger government has been growing right under our noses right here in Texas. All you have to do is add up the numbers . . . connect the dots and the story is eye opening.

Despite the fact that our state constitution was written and designed to make passing laws hard, rather than easy the Texas Legislature has managed to pass over 3,500 new laws during the previous two Texas Legislative sessions. This is serves as a clear indication that big government is alive and well in Texas. When you add this with the passage of the largest spending budget in Texas history this past May, 2013 and it becomes very clear to all that Texas government is becoming more and more like Washington, D.C. right in front of our eyes.

So it is only fair and reasonable for me to ask our Texas legislators who voted for the Texas budget of 2014-2015, "Was the passage of the state's largest spending budget in Texas history the result of "conservative leadership?" I certainly hope not because if that is the case Texas definitely can do without this kind of "conservative leadership in the future.

Now more than ever, Texas, as well as all states, need political leaders who will stand up and defend the constitution, safeguard our liberties, and fight for our traditional family and social values that define us as a nation. We need leaders who are bold and fearless in that charge and who are willing to do what is morally right and not what is politically beneficial. Anything less will not produce the results millions of people are asking for in states across America.

Let Me Be Clear

Government cannot and will not ever fix itself. You and I must take the leadership role in this quest to bring about change in our government at all levels: city, county, state, and federal. Government needs to be cleaned out and reformed. Good government has a vital role in a society, as a steward of common resources and public services, but it has clearly proven to the people of America and Texas it cannot deal effectively with the important challenges of today.

Today, government has become a bureaucratic cesspool of misguided, arrogant bureaucrats who have come to believe they rule the world and they know what is best for me, you, and all of society. This is the goal of the ideas and strategies found in *Winning Now*.

"No government ever voluntarily reduces itself in size. Government programs, once launched, never disappear. Actually, a government bureau is the nearest thing to eternal life we'll ever see on this earth!"— *Ronald Reagan*

Understanding the Legislative Process

*"Legislation can neither be wise nor just which seeks the welfare of
a single interest at the expense and to the injury of many and varied
interests."—Andrew Johnson*

In order to have an impact on your state legislature, you must have
a basic understanding how it is structure, how often it meets, and
who are the key decision makers that have the greatest impact
on the outcome of the legislative session each time the legislature
meets. For the purpose of this book I will focus primarily on
examining how the Texas legislature works.

The Make Up of the Texas Legislature

The Texas legislative process is governed by the Texas
Constitution, applicable statutes, and the rules of procedure of
the senate and house, and the different phases of activity typically
occur within a prescribed timetable. The rules of procedure are
adopted by the respective chambers at the beginning of each
session.[2]

The Texas Constitution divides state government into three
separate but equal branches: the executive branch headed by the
governor is the chief executive of the state and is elected for a four-
year term of office; the judicial branch, which consists of the Texas
Supreme Court and all state courts; and the legislative branch,
headed by the Texas Legislature.

The Texas Legislature is composed of 31 members in the Senate and 150 members in the House of Representatives. The Lieutenant Governor serves as the President of the Senate. Texas State senators are elected for four-year terms. State Representatives are elected for two year terms and at the beginning of each regular session, the first order of business that is conducted by the House of Representatives is to elect one of their members to serve as the Speaker of the House. The Speaker serves as presiding officer of the House for the next two years. Currently, all members of the Legislature are paid $600 per month plus state employee benefits.

The Legislature convenes for regular sessions on the second Tuesday of January during odd numbered years. The governor may call special sessions. Although not a frequent occurrence, special sessions have been called for major issues such as the state budget and educational school tax reform.

Executive

The Executive branch of state government is in charge of putting laws into effect and administering government functions. Offices under the Executive branch include the Governor, Lieutenant Governor, Attorney General, Land Commissioner, Comptroller of Public Accounts, State Board of Education members, and Railroad Commissioners.

Governor

The Governor is the head of the Executive branch of government and leader of the state. The Governor works with State Senators and Representatives to pass laws that will help the citizens of Texas. Before any bill can become law, it must pass through the Governor's office where it will be signed or vetoed. The Governor is the only person who has the power to call a special session, an additional period of time called after regular session that can last up to thirty days. The Governor must be at least 30 years old and a resident of Texas for five years before being elected.

The major executive powers of the governor are to execute the laws of the state, extradite fugitives from justice, serve as commander in chief of the military forces of the state, declare martial law, appoint numerous state officials, fill vacancies in state and district offices, call special elections to fill vacancies in the legislature, fill vacancies in the United States Senate until an election can be held, submit the budget to the legislature, and serve on several state boards.

Legislative

The Texas Legislature is the lawmaking branch of government. It is bicameral, meaning it is divided into two halves: the Texas House of Representatives and the Texas Senate. Both chambers have to make and approve the "rules" or laws that govern Texas. The time period in which the legislature convenes to pass new laws and handle state business is called the "legislative session." Regular legislative sessions begin in January of every odd-numbered year and convene for not more than 140 days. The Governor may call the legislature into special session as deemed appropriate. Special sessions are limited to issues specifically stated in the governor's call and may meet up to the 30-day maximum. The governor's call for special session is a list of specific priorities he deems necessary for the state to address.

Texas House Of Representatives

There are 150 members of the Texas House of Representatives elected for two-year terms, running for re-election in even-numbered years. As established by the Texas Constitution, members must be 21 years of age, a citizen of Texas for two years prior to election, and a resident of the district from which elected one year prior to election. Members of the House of Representatives are elected to two-year terms and currently, represent districts of about 172,000 people each.

The Speaker of the House is the presiding officer and key leader of the House, elected by a majority of House members. The Speaker's duties include maintaining order within the House, recognizing members during debate, and ruling on procedural matters, appointing chairmanships and members to committees, and sending bills for committee review. The Speaker may also appoint conference committee members, create select committees, and direct committees to conduct interim studies when the legislature is not in session. The Speaker Pro Tempore, appointed by the Speaker, is primarily a ceremonial position and presides over the House during its consideration of local and consent bills.

Bills are scheduled for consideration on the House floor by the Calendars Committee. A House member who is sponsoring a bill for debate on the floor goes to the front podium just below the speaker's desk to explain the bill. Other House members who wish to ask questions or make a point pertaining to the measure go to the podium at the rear of the chamber, known as the "back microphone." The Speaker must rise to put a question before the House prior to a vote. The Speaker has the same right as other House members to vote, but may withhold action in order to cast the deciding vote or break a tie.

Senate

The Senate is made up of 31 senators. As established by the Texas Constitution, a senator must be at least 26 years of age, a citizen of Texas five years prior to election, and a resident of the district from which elected one year prior to election. Each senator serves a four-year term—one half of the Senate membership is elected every two years. Senators represent senate districts of about 800,000 people. Since 2011 one Senate district has more people than a U.S. Congressional district.

As presiding officer of the Senate, the Lieutenant Governor is officially called the President of the Senate. The Lieutenant Governor is elected by a statewide popular vote to serve a four-year term. The Lieutenant Governor is not a member of the Senate, and votes only in the case of a tie. The Lieutenant Governor appoints all chairs and members of the Senate committees, and refers all bills to committee.

The Lieutenant Governor also schedules most bills for consideration on the Senate floor. Bills which are local or uncontested are scheduled by the Senate Administration Committee. The President Pro Tempore is considered the second most powerful position, and can be reserved to any political party in the chamber without regard as to what party is in the majority. President Pro Tempores are usually the most senior members of the Senate. The President Pro Tempore preside when the Lieutenant Governor is not present or when the legislature is not in regular session.

The Senate holds the power of advice and consent on gubernatorial appointments to state boards and commissions.

The Process of Passing Legislation In Texas

The procedure by which laws are adopted are governed by the Texas Constitution and by rules adopted by each house (the House of Representatives and Senate) of the legislature at the beginning of each session. The Texas Constitution requires that a bill must be read on three separate days in each house before it can become effective.

The first reading of a bill occurs when the bill is introduced and referred to a committee. Many bills are not reported by a committee and are considered "dead" for the session. Second reading occurs when the bill has been heard by a committee, favorably reported, the author has moved that all necessary rules be suspended to consider the bill on the floor, and members have approved the motion by the requisite vote. In order for a bill to be read the third time on the same calendar day, an affirmative vote of four-fifths of the members present is required.

If a House bill is amended by the Senate, or a Senate bill is amended by the House, the bill is returned to the house of origin for concurrence on the amendments or the appointment of a conference committee to adjust the differences between the House and Senate versions of the bill.

When a bill is finally approved by both houses, it is enrolled in final form, signed by the presiding officers of both houses, and sent to the governor. Within 10 days after receiving the bill, the governor may approve the bill by signing it or may veto the bill and return it to the house of origin with a statement of objections. If the governor fails to either sign or veto a bill in 10 days of a session, the governor has 20 days after the end of the session to sign or veto the bill. A vetoed bill may be passed over the governor's objection by an affirmative two thirds vote of both houses.[2]

Here is how the legislative process works in Texas

- How a bill originates
- Introducing a bill
- Referral to a committee
- The committee process
- House calendars and list of items eligible
- Senate agenda and intent calendar
- Floor action
- Consideration of local and noncontroversial bills
- Return of bill to originating chamber
- Conference committee
- Governor's action
- Effective date
- Filing and publication of laws

For more information about the legislative process visit the Guide to Texas Legislative Information website located at http://www.tlc. state.tx.us/gtli/legproc/process.html.

The lawmaking process involves four major stages: introduction, committee action, floor action, and enrollment. In a bicameral legislature like Texas, with a House and a Senate, the first three stages must occur in each of the houses consecutively. After the house in which the bill is introduced completes action on the measure, the bill is sent to the second house, where the process is repeated through the three stages. The fourth stage, enrollment, occurs in the originating house after both houses have agreed on the final form of the proposal.

Word of Caution

Our Texas Constitution makes it very difficult to pass a law. In fact, there is a saying I once heard from an experience House member on the House Floor. He said, "The Senate is the place were bills go and die." How true this is in Texas.

One word of caution that needs your attention. Passing laws should not be the goal of every legislator. I learned that at the end of my first term in office. If we truly believe that government should be limited then the goal of a "conservative" lawmaker is to ensure that conservative principles are pursued at every given opportunity. That includes in the passage of laws.

Consider the state of Texas the past two legislative sessions. The Texas Legislature has passed over 3.500 bills during these two sessions. What troubles me is that the Republican Party, the party of limited government, has been in control of all the Legislative branches since 2003 and they continue to allow the passage of thousands of new laws every time it meets. When you factor in the administrative costs associated with most of these new laws you quickly conclude that government isn't shrinking in Texas, rather it is growing at an alarming rate.

According to the *Republican Party Platform*, the Party is dedicated to the cause of limited government. The Platform specially states and I quote, "RESERVING AMERICAN FREEDOM LIMITING THE EXPANSE OF GOVERNMENT POWER." Yet, I am afraid that many of our state leaders don't seem to adhere to all this and many other conservative principles stated in the party platform. Now, that in itself is a problem, but perhaps a greater problem is that we the people continue to re-elect legislators who do not govern in the same way they campaign.

In conclusion, if this is what conservative government looks like I wonder what the next 10 years are going to look like. You and I that we must always be sober and diligent in our quest for keeping government in check. It is a never ending task that if we shut our eyes for just a moment government will do what it does best and that is to continue to grow. It is a beast whose hunger is never quenched.

"You do not examine legislation in the light of the benefits it will convey if properly administered, but in the light of the wrongs it would do and the harms it would cause if improperly administered."—Lyndon B. Johnson

Diagram of Process For Passing A Bill In Texas Legislature

This diagram displays the sequential flow of a bill from the time it is introduced in the House of Representatives to final passage and transmittal to the governor.[3]

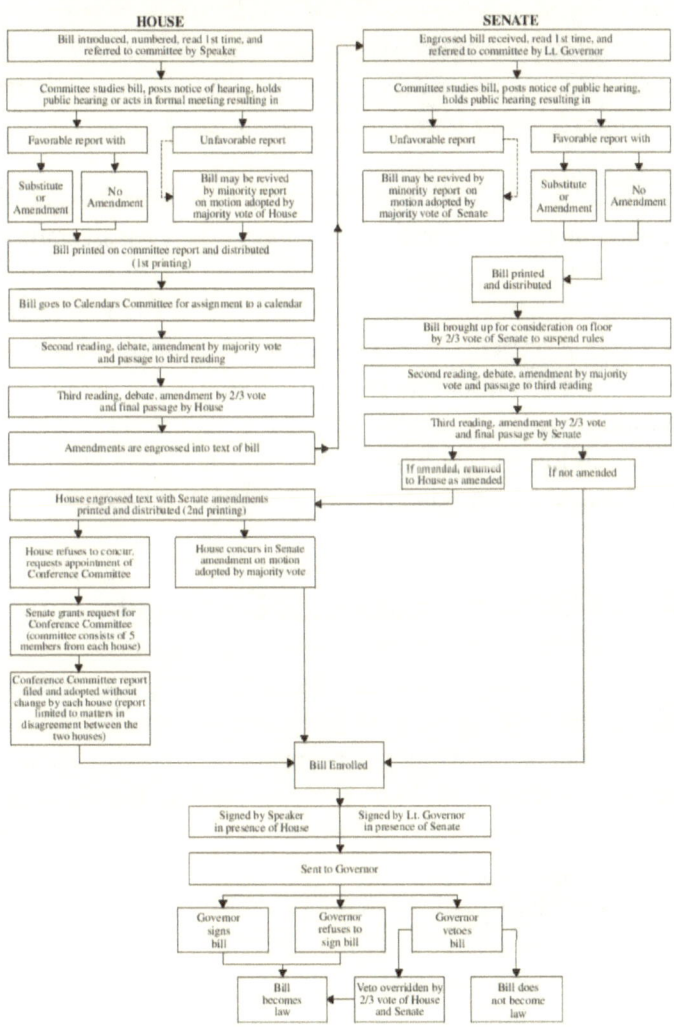

The Texas Legislative Process for House Bills and Resolutions

This diagram displays the sequential flow of a bill from the time it is introduced in the house of representatives to final passage and transmittal to the governor.

Achieving Excellence In Government Takes Work

"A wise and frugal Government, which shall restrain men from injuring one another, shall leave them otherwise free to regulate their own pursuits of industry and improvement, and shall not take from the mouth of labor the bread it has earned."—Thomas Jefferson

Now that you have a good understanding of your state's legislative process, your next step is to form and organize your grassroots campaign and team members with the intent purpose of pursing perfection in government. Success in the political arena usually requires a group of people working together to bring about change. I highly recommend that you get other likeminded people to join your crusade if winning is what you really want to accomplish. This will be followed by identifying what issues you wish to pursue with your legislators and during the legislative session.

Creating an Effective Grassroots Campaign

Many times during my career as a certified public accountant, I often encountered individuals and business owners who knew they needed to change some aspect of their tax or financial life because of a goal or plan they had. The problem was that for many of them they just didn't know how to go about it nor did they know what questions to ask to so they could the things they needed to do in order to achieve their goals or plan.

During my first legislative session serving in the Texas Legislature in 2011, I found myself in the same predicament as many of my clients. In the beginning I didn't know what questions to ask, or who the main people were. I didn't know the legislative process nor did I know about the many traditions that were observed in the Texas House of Representatives. I didn't know the rules and I didn't know who I could trust. All I knew was that I wanted to provide common sense, proven solutions to address the many legislative challenges facing our state. I wrote this book so I could share what I have learned as a private citizen, business owner, and as a legislator.

Winning Now is about providing the average citizen the answers to many of the questions that often are asked by those who wish to change public policy. "Winning Now" is an effective roadmap to bring about change in local, state and federal government. The ideas and information provided in this book directed to the everyday American who is concerned about our country and wish to take charge of their city, state, or federal government legislative agenda. If you want to be in the driver's seat to affect public policy, then *Winning Now* is for you.

Winning Now offers only a handful of common sense, proven strategies to many of the problems that have historically plagued states across America. Yet, because of the different political ideologies that are often found present in state legislatures there is an inherent challenge of finding consensus or agreement during the legislative process. But, with the right tools and the right message, there is a high probability of finding bi-partisan support for many legislative ideas.

Therefore, our journey to transform local, state or federal government is a long and difficult one. Your best weapons will be truth, knowledge, a positive attitude, good communication skills and the most important one of them all, persistence.

Defining the Elements of Efficient and Effective Government

I first heard the phrase "good government" in 2006 in Nueces County during one of our many local Republican Party strategy sessions. We were discussing the idea of messaging as we discussed how the Republican Party would prepare for the 2006 Mid-Term elections when a good friend of mine, Michael Bergsma, recommended that we consider using the phrase, "good government." We were trying to find the right message to convey to the general public about what were the key values of the Republican Party in Nueces County. That's when I came to learn the lesson that words have meaning and the fewer the words we use to describe something, the more people will listen and understand the message. This concept was so powerful, that I believe it changed the political landscape in Nueces County.

"The basis of effective government is public confidence, and that confidence is endangered when ethical standards falter or appear to falter."—John F. Kennedy

For the first time since the Reconstruction Era of the 1860's, Nueces County elected its first Republican County Judge in 2006. In addition, we also elected our first Republican Sheriff since 1925. The powerful, but simple message, "good government" was so clear. It was so easy to understand that for the first time in my lifetime, the general public in Nueces County clearly understood what the Republican Party stood for and it showed at the polls. But, it didn't stop there.

Despite major Republican losses at all levels during the 2006 Mid-Term elections and the 2008 General Elections all across America, the victories that we experienced in Nueces County in 2006 helped pave the way for more Republican victories in 2008 and 2010. In fact, in 2010 we won every Republican race in Nueces County except for two races.

Political winners are those who can communicate a simple phrase like "good government" to reach the hearts and minds of the majority of voters. This concept is a fundamental principle in building an effective organization. With this kind of message we can communicate a vision that translates into values that touches and moves the emotions of voters. These values represent hope and opportunity and people are desperate for hope because it is sorely lacking in American politics today.

Good government is what the majority of Americans want. These are the key elements we find in our U.S. Constitution and in our Declaration of Independence. Therefore, the elements of good government are a government that works for the people, is made up of the people, and is run and directed by the people." This means it is a government that is more efficient and more effective with your tax dollars. It is a government that is accountable, responsible and, delivers measurable results. It is a government that will listen to you. It is a government that will stand up for your conservative values, not sacrifice them.

A NBC/Wall Street Journal poll released on July 24, 2013 found that Americans' disapproval of Congress has reached unprecedented levels, while approval of President Barack Obama has dropped significantly to 46 percent. According to the survey, 83 percent of Americans disapprove of the job Congress is doing in Washington, an all-time high in the poll. Just 12 percent approve of Congress' job, while 57 percent they would replace every member of Congress if they could.[4]

Today, more than ever American are looking for leaders who can create a vision and be able to communicate that vision in a simple, easy to understand positive message. However, in order to make this concept work, it requires you to get your grassroots movement involved in all aspects of the political and governing process with a clear understanding of the process and with a clear set of measurable, obtainable objectives.

"A Government of the people, by the people and for the people, shall not perish from the earth."—Abraham Lincoln

You Must Become A Game Changer of Policy

One of the most important people involved in the transformation of government is you. You must become what I will refer to as "a Game Changer." Game Changers are people who are different than the rest of society. "They are wired differently, their DNA is different," said Tom Harrison, Chairman of Diversified Agency Services. The moderately successful person focuses on the roadblocks and how to get over or around them. A Game Changer focuses on the end goal. Game Changers look at problems or challenges as opportunities and these opportunities have no limits, therefore no box to restrict their thinking. They look not as how things are, but rather as how they should be. Transforming state government means raising the bar for evaluating our political leaders' performance and the decisions they make. It means requiring politicians to keep their campaign promises. I means that government meet higher fiscal accountability standards. It means redefining the core mission for state government.

"I think every American has a role in saving this country. Whether you're Democrat, Republican, independent, it doesn't matter. We all know the country's in trouble. We may disagree on how to solve it, but we all know the country's in trouble".—Glenn Beck

Game Changers do not make excuses. They live for the opportunity to change what government is into what it should be. Game Changers understand the power of words and therefore, are persistent in staying the course with a powerful message based on facts, truth, and common sense. The words they use must be simple, capable of emotionally connecting with the average, hardworking American family.

Once a person decides to be a Game Changer, their next step is to identify other like-minded individuals. Together, they begin their mission by engaging and inspiring people who are actively involved in the many different grass root organizations in their community who know the political process and have contacts in leadership positions. The idea of engaging people requires for us to be effective communicators. This may require special training or practice, but there is no other way.

The Power of Words

"I've learned that people will forget what you said, people will forget what you did, but people will never forget how you made them feel."—Maya Angelou

In the world of politics and government, words have real meaning. Often, one word or one statement said at the wrong place or at the wrong time can derail a promising political career or can destroy a winning campaign. All over the political landscape elected leaders hire so called "experts" or communication directors. The corporate world calls these people their Public Affairs Director. Regardless of their title, the role these people play and the importance of what they do cannot be under estimated. The lesson for us who desire to have an excellent government is to learn this skill well or hire someone who can do the job for us.

Most people are not born as effective communicators. Rather, most of them become effective because of hard work, education and practice. The value of communication cannot be under estimated. The master communicator of all time, Jesus Christ, spoke like no other man. He left us a model to follow. Reading the Gospels we learn how Jesus communicated with words. He spoke in parables to teach important divine principles and he often told stories that captured the audience's attention and revealed an important life lessons. At times he spoke softly and at other times he spoke firmly. He time he chose his words carefully because Jesus understood that the words we use in our communications are powerful and capable of changing lives of both friends and enemies. Consider these attributes of using the proper words when communicating:

- Words communicate powerful ideas
- Words reveal our character
- Words change lives
- Words can shape our future

People who seek to influence others must never forget the power of the words they use. For in the words we choose, we determine the influence we have over others. If you want to learn more about how to communicate effectively I highly recommend the book written by Dr. Frank Lutz titled, *Wining*. Mr. Lutz writes these sobering words in the first chapter of his book, "So before you go any further, ask yourself two simple questions: First, how badly do you want to win? And second, are you willing to do what it takes to move from the ordinary to the extraordinary? If the answers are both yes, then let's begin."[5]

Game Changers find ways to prevail over the many naysayers and critics who will gather in force to silence them and discredit all they do. The critics will often have more resources and will often have the help of the mainstream media to accomplish their goal of diminishing your voice as you begin to make progress in influencing many participants of the governing process. You will be required to engage, communicate, persist on your good government objectives, and in due time if you don't quit you will prevail.

There is also another very important principle you must never forget. There are two things that motivate state legislators: (1) they all pay attention to what the voters in their district have to say and (2) they are greatly motivated by campaign donations.

Therefore, unless you have some serious money to contribute the one tool you have left to gain the legislators' attention is to be very vocal and very persistent in your requests and communications with them. The more vocal you are the more the legislators will listen to you. This is critical to your success.

Another key principle you must embrace is for you to never give up, never accept defeat in this kind of endeavor. You must be willing to work as long and as hard as it takes to get the job done right. As you go through these *Winning Now* strategies, the legislative victories you seek often come in smaller, less than expected, gains. It is the primary way legislative changes occur in state houses throughout America.

To be successful as a Game Changer you must possess a positive attitude and you must be willing to accept, temporarily, small size gains. Big, bold ideas often take many legislative sessions to successfully pass both houses of the state's legislature. When this occurs don't be disappointment. Rather, this means you are doing the right things. This is just the way things work in most cases. To expect more is to set yourself up for great disappointment.

We The People Do Extraordinary Things

If you have any doubts about your ability to succeed allow me to remind you that you come from a long line of people who have done great things in our nation's history. For the past 230 years Americans have accomplished great things. Let us remember that any greatness credited to America belongs to the 325 million citizens who make up the first three words in our Constitution: ``We the People."

It was "We the People" who endured and overcame the great challenges in our nation's history. It was "We the People who overcame and endured wars, a depression, and a cold war. It was "We the People" whose courage and sacrifices lifted us from the depths of national calamity, labored to rebuild our mighty economic strength, and led the way to restoring our respect once again in the world.

Yes, it was "We the People," that were an extraordinary breed of people the world has come to call Americans. So today it is the duty of our generation to take the torch of our ancestors and become the heroes for the next generation. Today, we are called upon to be the courageous, the doers, the dreamers, and the builders of today as we work, build, defend, and sacrifice our fortunes, our duty, and our honor to uphold and maintain this glorious experiment in democracy the world calls America.

"Freedom is never more than one generation away from extinction. We didn't pass it to our children in the bloodstream. It must be fought for, protected, and handed on for them to do the same."—Ronald Reagan

Rebuilding the Public Trust

"We need transparency in government spending. We need to put each government expenditure online so every Floridian can see where their tax money is being spent"—Senator Marco Rubio

One of the most alarming problems that exist in America is that the American public does not trust their government. There is a reason for this. Let's take a journey back into time to see what transpired that perhaps are the reasons why most Americans do not trust their government and that will be followed by what I believe are some simple ideas government must implement to regain the trust of the American people.

People Want To Trust In America

I remember back in January 2009 as Barack Obama was about to take the oath of office, he reminded the American people of his vision of hope and change that would transform the American society.

The election of 2008 was a clear mandate from the American people for the next President to fix many of the problems that were causing us great economic harm and we wanted him to provide the leadership to improve the economy, fix the financial meltdown of our banking system, to increase access to health care while restraining costs, and to reduce energy costs and our dependence on oil, among others.

In addition, America was fighting two wars. One was in Iraq and the other was in Afghanistan. The high cost of the two wars and the meltdown of our financial markets resulted in a significant increase in bankruptcies, home foreclosures, and a bank closures all over America. Jobs were being lost in a rapid pace, families were hurting and America begin its worst recession since the days of the Great Depression.

These hardships resulted in the American people deeply losing confidence in the federal government. This made the 2008 Presidential Election an extremely critical election because the next President ability to successfully resolves these problems would be the difference as to whether the American people would recognize their government as one being trustworthy or not.

In fact, I remember President Obama state in his Inauguration Speech that he was going to open up Washington and that his administration was going to be the most transparent in American history. People were hopeful and excited, and since that time the President and our Congress have failed to gain public trust.

A Brief History of America's Trust in Government

William Galston, who is the Senior Fellow in Governance Studies at the Brookings Institution, wrote in an article titled: *Rebuilding Public Trust in Government: Where We've Been, Where We Are, Where We Need to Go*, that the history of public trust has evolved to its current state of being due to a series of key moments in history. He said,

> "Looking back to the late 1950s, we can see that the federal government that fought the Great Depression, won the Second World War, avoided the anticipated post-war economic slump, built the interstate highway system, and encouraged the growth of a mass middle class had the opportunity to draw upon a huge reservoir of public support."[6]

Looking back, in 1958, 73 percent of the American people reported that they trusted the government in Washington to do what was right most of the time. The 76 percent of the electorate that gave Lyndon Johnson his 1964 landslide said the same thing which was the highest percentage ever achieved in American history.[6]

During the next 10 years, public trust declined to 61 percent; by 1972, to 53 percent. Scholars point to Vietnam, assassinations, and racial and cultural conflict as the major contributors to the 23-point drop in the eight years between 1964 and the 1972 Nixon landslide over McGovern. Then came the Watergate affair, which dealt a shattering blow to public trust. By the midterm election of 1974, it had plunged an additional 17 points, to 36 percent—less than half the peak attained just ten years earlier.[6]

According to Mr. Galston America's public trust never fully recovered after Watergate. This is not to say that trust has remained constant over the past 36 years. A quick look at history reveals that mistrust in government continued to decline during the Ford-Carter years, bottoming out at 25 percent in 1980. Mr. Galston said,

> "It rose through much of the 1980s, reaching 44 percent the day of the Reagan 1984 landslide. It still stood at 40 percent the day George H. W. Bush defeated Michael Dukakis. Then it slid again, to 29 percent on Election Day 1992 and a sorrowful 21 percent in 1994 as Republicans ended the Democrats' 40-year majority in the House of Representatives."[6]

In the ten years from the 1994 midterms to George W. Bush's 2004 re-election, trust rebounded. By the end of the Clinton administration, it had more than doubled from its low-point, to 44 percent, identical to the Reagan-era peak, and consistent with the proposition that trust in government often follows in the same direction as the state of the economy. Another pattern that is noticeable is that people tend to rally around the government in the face of a national threat such as war. After the 9/11 event public trust increased to 56 percent. By November 2004 it settled back down to 47 percent.[6]

During President there was another drop in public trust for two reasons. First, because the President was unable to find weapons of mass destruction which was the reason cited by the President for initiating the Iraq war, and second, because the economy entered a deep recession after the near-collapse of the financial system that began in late 2007. By Election Day 2008, it had declined 17 points, to just 30 percent. [6]

Despite the hope and change that Barack Obama's victorious campaign had inspired, there is no evidence that it changed the public's attitude toward the federal government. In June of 2009, despite Obama's overwhelming approval rating of more than 60 percent of the American people, only 20 percent of Americans said they trusted the government; a number that has not improved very much to this day.[6]

Finally, Mr. Golston writes,

> "Mistrust of government is not confined to our national institutions. Unlike some previous periods in which public regard for state and local government remained high even as trust in the national government tumbled, all levels of the federal system are now in the same boat. In 1997, 50 percent of Americans thought that the national government was having a positive impact on their lives, versus only 38 percent today."[6]

According to physiologists, public trust has three key dimensions. To trust, we must believe that individuals and institutions have the competence to deliver the results they have undertaken to produce. To trust we must also believe that they have integrity— that they mean what they say and that their promises are sincere. Competence without integrity is not enough to maintain trust, as Richard Nixon discovered when he was President. In addition, public trust is closely tied to ability, as Jimmy Carter learned during his Presidency.[6]

The third key determinant of public trust is responsiveness.[6] We the people must believe that the government is genuinely listening to us and working on the problems we believe are the most important to us. When this takes place public trust tends to rise rapidly.

From the current state of affairs it would be wise for our elected leaders to heed the many lessons we can learn from history. The American people almost always will respond favorably to any politician who will to listen to their plea for real, common sense solutions to our country's most important issues. The American people want less politics and rhetoric. They want measurable results. They want their leaders to be honest by telling them the truth about the problems we have and the proposed solutions they recommend. When elected leaders do more to listen to the public, slowly but surely public trust becomes evident. Once when Ronald Reagan was being briefed about some polling data in regards to a particular issue he responded to his staff, "Let's do the right thing and the good politics will follow." How right he was.

"Public officers are the servants and agents of the people, to execute laws which the people have made and within the limits of a constitution which they have established."—Steven Grover Cleveland

Trust In Government Begins With Increasing Transparency

There is a direct correlation between public trust and better economic and social results. Governments that make more information about policy intentions and enactment is the primary key element of achieving excellence in government. This process begins with the budget. The budget is the single most important policy document of any government entity. If you have a flawed budget process then a bad budget will be adopted. If the budget process is focused on the proper priorities of government spending then the budget should serve as a well-designed roadmap for government.

Therefore, budget transparency is defined as the full disclosure of all relevant fiscal information in a timely and systematic manner and in a format that benefits the public. Since the budget is the most important document in building public trust then all government leaders should demand that the budget be written in a clear, easy to understand format. In Texas, the state budget is not easy to understand because it is not written in conformity with general accepted accounting principles.

According to a survey conducted by the Pew Center on the States and the Public Policy Institute of California in 2010, nearly 66 percent of the American people stated they never have trusted government to do what is right.[7] From the response it's clear to see that the American public is demanding more proof that their government is responding to their needs and desires. Government must fundamentally change how it conducts business and how it provides information in the public arena in a simple, easy to understand format if trust is to ever be rebuild with its citizens. In order to achieve excellence in government we must take the proper steps to rebuild public trust.[7]

"If we want to truly regain the public's trust, we can provide greater accountability and transparency with a simple step. Let's start by communicating to our constituents about the votes we take."—Melissa Bean, U.S. Representative

Many states have taken the lead in addressing this issue. The Texas Comptroller of Public Accounts launched the Texas Comptroller Leadership Circle program in December 2009 to recognize local governments across Texas that are striving to meet a high standard for financial transparency online. This bold approach in transparency addresses a positive step in the right direction if government is ever going to regain the public trust they have lost over the years.

Taxpayers have the right to know that their governments—whether at the federal, state or local level—is spending their hard earned tax dollars prudently and wisely. These efforts to open Texas government spending to the general public via the Comptroller's website is now setting new, high standards of accountability and financial integrity across all levels of government in Texas. The downside to this highly acclaim effort is that it has no enforcement mechanism for compliance. Therefore, many local government entities and school districts have chosen not to participate in this effort to make government more transparent.

These efforts by the Texas Comptroller of Public Accounts office serves as a role model of transparency and open government for the other states in America. As such, many other states have taken measures to address their transparency issues.

Support for government transparency is strong. For example, Michigan and Texas both considered legislation that would ban electronic communications during public meetings. These actions appear to signal a growing understanding that while texting, tweets, email and blog posts may make for easier and more rapid communications, there still remain a growing mistrust in government officials not disclosing the content of these electronic messages thereby, creating a lack of true transparency.[8]

Another three examples can be found in the states of Nevada, New Jersey and Virginia. The state of Nevada recently enacted a new law to provide more information on the Internet about the quality of patient care, incident of infection and patient re-admissions.[9]

In 2011 the state of New Jersey considered a measure that would have required government agencies and state authorities to have an online presence. The measure came after a report was released by the state comptroller showed that only one third of agencies and authorities shared information with the public about their activities.

Finally, the state of Virginia started streaming its Transportation Boards and Commissions meetings live online. The initiative is part of the state's open government plan by showing the full meeting instead of just posting minutes. "Virginians interested in witnessing the important work that takes place during these meetings can log on to their laptops, PCs or smart phones for easy access," stated Governor Bob McDonnell. "Open government is better government. I am pleased that we are capitalizing on this technology to give even greater access to these public events."[10]

In the book, *How Technology Can Make Government Better, Democracy Stronger, and Citizens More Powerful*, author Beth Simone Noveck, states, "The central theme is that we need to rethink democracy in the digital age." According to Noveck, using technology in improve transparency will result in stronger public decision-making capabilities by the decision makers because it will connect the power of the many to the work of the few. "The private sector has learned that better decision making requires looking beyond institutionalized centers of expertise," said Noveck. "Now it's time for government to do the same."

The more we look out into the future the more we must conclude that technology is the key that can allow for more transparency and thereby greatly improve our efforts to rebuild public trust once again in America. Technology will allow for government to share their knowledge and expertise with anyone 24 hours a day seven days a week. By making government more accessible to the public we can begin to better understand how government functions, what are the real problems and better understand what our elected leaders plan to do to solve today's most complex problems.[11]

When we bring government together with the people, we produce an outcome that President Abraham Lincoln saw when he concluded the Gettysburg Address with these words,

> ". . . that we here highly resolve that these dead shall not have died in vain—that this nation, under God, shall have a new birth of freedom—and that government of the people, by the people, for the people, shall not perish from the earth."

Practical Tools To Improve Transparency

What are some basic elements of government transparency? According to legislative experts, here are three things that should be implemented at the state level to improve government transparency:

- Create a Transparent Budget Web site
- Adopt a 72-Hour Budget Timeout
- Require Fiscal Notes Before Action on Spending Bills

Since state lawmakers spend billions each budget cycle, taxpayers deserve a government that will be responsive, accountable and that can deliver measurable results on a regular basis. Taxpayers should be able to get answers quickly and conveniently. This is especially true since modern technology makes accessing large amounts of information east to do.

Create a Transparent Budget Website

Sooner or later, most citizens wonder, "Just how, when, and where does the state government spend our tax dollars?" Other frequent questions often asked are, "What do our elected representatives want to accomplish when they spend public money, and what results are actually achieved?" These and many other questions deserve an honest answer to be given to the public.

Since 2007, The American Legislative Executive Council (ALEC) has recommend states to adopt and implement ALEC's model "Taxpayer Transparency Act." The Act requires that state governments setup and maintain a searchable budget website to show citizens where their tax dollars are spent and for what purpose. Among the types of information typically included on such sites are:[12]

- State expenditures by fund or account.
- Expenditures by agency, program, and sub-program.
- State revenues by source.
- State expenditures by budget object and sub-object.
- State agency workloads, caseloads, and performance measurements.
- Historical information on state spending as well as access to state service contracts.

The costs associated with the implementation of a website that makes available more information to the public are minimal compared to the benefits it provides. For example, the state of Nebraska placed its expenditures online for $37,000, down from a previous $1.3 million price tag. The state of Oklahoma implemented budget transparency at minimal cost to taxpayers. In the state of Texas, we implemented Open Book Texas, a database similar to the one called for in ALEC's Taxpayer Transparency Act. This resulted in a savings of $8.6 million.[12]

Besides the benefit of educating and opening the books of state government to the general public and thereby improving the public's trust in their government, there is another great benefit to be gained from the implementation of a transparent budget website. It will serve as an asset to policymakers and agencies to assist them in identifying and eliminating waste and inefficiencies in their expenditures. How about that? Now that is excellence in government.

As a CPA, I strongly believe that it is important for you, the taxpayers, to have detailed information about how your money is spent. However, in order for these reforms to take place, you must demand them from your city, state, and federal legislators because they will not voluntarily want to open up the records to what they have been up to over the past few years. If your state has not implemented ALEC's Taxpayer Transparency Act now would be a great time to begin that process. For more information on this program go to ALEC's website at www.alec.org.

Adopt a 72-Hour Budget review period

Do you remember back in the spring of 2010 when Congress was considering President Obama's Health Care legislation? This was one of the most important pieces of legislation this country has ever considered by the Congress. Yet, it was during that contested debate in Washington D.C. that House Speaker Nancy Pelosi (D-CA), said her famous words, "We have to pass the bill so that you can find out what is in it." This is the same Nancy Pelosi who, only weeks earlier, was bragging about the transparency of the process that produced the bill that was at time stalled in Congress.

This is the same Speaker Pelosi who brushed aside concerns raised by organizations all over America that members of Congress should actually commit to reading the bill before voting for it and that it be posted online for at least 72 hours before any vote by Congress so that the American people can have an opportunity to read it and provide the public feedback on that particular piece of legislation. This is a perfect example of why we desperately need transparency in government.

During the 2011 Texas Legislature our budget bill HB1, was over 400 pages long. Taking into consideration the fact that a state's combined budget (operating, capital, and transportation) often can be hundreds of pages long it is prudent and necessary that state governments implement a waiting period to vote on important legislation such as a state budget bill. Allowing an opportunity for a detailed review by the public prior to hearings or votes on budget bills would help increase public trust in government and enhance accountability for the spending decisions being made.

The good news is this principle is already in place for Texas, but there others states that do not. If your state currently does not have a 72-hour timeout period for all legislators and citizens to read the bill before it comes up for a vote, then now is the time to present and move forward with this idea.

Require Fiscal Notes

One of the questions most often used in the business world is, "What is the cost or impact of our decision?" You and I would think that understanding the financial impact would be standard operating procedure for most legislative decision makers. However, this is not always the case when it comes to government decision makers.

In Texas, fiscal notes are required in order to hear a bill in committee or on the House floor for debate. The Texas Legislature requires this because it provides legislators and the public vital information regarding the financial impact in any proposed piece of legislation. However, in several states bills are introduced and voted on before the data on fiscal repercussions are made available to those voting on the bills. State officials can easily pretend to be surprised at the state of the budget when it is obvious that the long-term budget forecasts have either been unseen or utterly disregarded.

All state officials and the public should know the full impact of a piece of legislation before any vote is taken. Bills proposing increased spending should not be considered for a hearing in committee until a completed fiscal note is available. The purpose of this recommendation is to ensure that wasteful spending bills cannot be pushed through the legislative bodies without the full fiscal consequences being made known to legislators and the public.

This practice is in line with demanding more transparency and accountability from state officials.

"We might hope to see the finances of the Union as clear and intelligible as a merchant's books, so that every member of Congress and every man of any mind in the Union should be able to comprehend them, to investigate abuses, and consequently, to control them."—Thomas Jefferson

"We do not have a functioning market in the true sense of the word in health care. That's a layer of transparency that's sorely needed in America."—Paul Ryan

Tools to Control Spending In Government

"An economy hampered by restrictive tax rates will never produce enough revenue to balance our budget, just as it will never produce enough jobs or enough profits."—John F. Kennedy

The Budget Process Is the Key

Not since the Great Depression of the 1930's had our nation faced a fiscal crisis as we did beginning in 2008. What we learned from this past recession is that the traditional way of managing and balancing the budget for state government was no longer an effective process. In the 2012-13 budget the Legislature balanced the budget by eliminating $15 billion from the previous budget amount. Then in the 2014-2015 budget passed in May, 2013 the Texas Legislature ended up spending $22 billion more than the 2012-13 budget.

Due to the wide swing in the availability of certified funds for the budget it is my professional opinion that Texas and other state governments must replace the current budget process with a zero base budget process to ensure that the budget spends its limited funds on the most important budget items.

The zero base budget process will eliminate the use of tricky accounting methods that have been used by the Texas Legislature for many years. In other words, the tricks of the past—increasing deficits, borrowing against anticipated revenues or underfunding pensions have all contributed to the financial mess Texas and many states throughout America find themselves in today.

As we enter our fifth year of this national recession that has gripped America since 2008, no segment of any government or public sector has been spared the financial challenges of dealing with a reduction of revenues and the increased demand for state and local government services. In addition to having to cope with budget cuts and increased populations, some states such as Texas, have also had to deal with increased regulatory requirements as well as having to cope with the issue of public safety as each day foreign threats loom across the Texas border in Mexico.

Therefore, government entities of all sizes are being forced to balance their budgets by either raising taxes or cutting spending. This will often result in the reduction of public services that many people depend on for meeting many of their basic needs while many others take them for granted and choose to stay home rather than find a job, any job.

For most legislatures, the most important issue in the near future will be to reduce spending and streamline state government to live within its means. Some have already begun to do just that. For example, Indiana Governor Mitch Daniels has been reining in spending since he took over in 2005, forcing agencies and local governments to look more carefully at what they do and how they do it. In 2011, Texas Legislature and Governor Rick Perry approved a budget that cut the state's spending by $15 billion. Texas like many other states have taken on state spending with a new attitude. I believe that if state could avoid approving budgets that cut spending then most states would not voluntarily do so, but do to the circumstances states are being forced to rethink how they balance their budgets.

Competitiveness is critical to every state's long-term future. States today compete not only against each other for jobs and talent but also against China, India, Mexico, and other countries. For states determined to move beyond their hard times they must accept change and implement a new way to run government in their respective states. They'll need to focus on competitiveness boosters like revitalizing infrastructure, pursuing radical education reform and reinventing economic development.

"As I have traveled throughout my Congressional district, the one thing I heard loud and clear was simply please stop spending money you do not have, rein in spending, live within a budget."—Tim Scott

Adopt Priority Based Budgeting

Perhaps the most important step in gaining control of state spending requires state leaders to adopt a budget methodology called "Priority-based budgeting." This requires all state officials and the state's citizens to first determine the core functions of government. While this may seem like an elementary step, it is seldom taken before legislative appropriations process is begun. In order to adopt a Priority-based budget," leaders and citizens must first ask the following questions:[12]

- What is the role of government?
- What is the essential services government must provide to fulfill its purpose?
- How will we know if the government is doing a good job?
- What should all of this cost?
- When cuts must be made, how will they be *properly* prioritized?

Only by carefully considering the proper role of government can legislators do an effective job of protecting individual rights, while providing essential services to taxpayers in an efficient, cost-effective manner.

By asking these vital questions, we take a common sense approach toward solving the question, "Where should we spend our tax dollars?" This step will ensure that what government is supposed to do will be done. Only when government focuses on the true core functions of government, can great savings be obtained as well as ensure that the services to be provided will be done at a lower cost to the taxpayers.

In order to define what should be the core functions of government, legislators and citizens should look to their state constitution. This is key to the process of reducing spending. Keep in mind that state lawmakers swear to uphold, protect and defend their federal and state constitutions. According to ALEC, when legislators are deciding what the core functions of government are, the following questions should be asked:

- Is this a proper function of government, or is it best left to the individual (family) or charitable organization?
- If the proposed function or activity is determined to be necessary, is it best left to local government which is closer to the people?
- Does it further increase taxes, regulations, or the size of government? If so, is this justified? [13]

39

Let me finish by saying that ultimately it is the responsibility of lawmakers to be honest with their citizens in every aspect of state government. However, developing a meaningful set of core governing principles requires lots of hard work, time, and courage to demand more from your state government. That is why it is up to you to ensure your state is transformed. Despite the many benefits of incorporating a new set of tools into the budget process or the many benefits of adopting a priority-based budgeting program, there will always be those state officials who will vigorously oppose or undermine any efforts to change the manner in which the state budget is written. Your job is to not allow them to have their way.

"A budget should reflect the values and priorities of our nation and its people."—Mary Landrieu

Adopt An Affective State Spending Limit

There is one last important component to the budget that needs to be in place at the state level if your state is to be transformed. It is to adopt an effective state spending limit. This legislature measure should be incorporated into the state constitution to ensure its longevity. Currently, many states have attempted to maintain some sort of spending limit or rainy day fund, but their effectiveness varies significantly. In Texas, we have a vaguely worded constitutional amendment, but it is totally ineffective in achieving its purpose. Despite many efforts to fix this problem, over the years many legislators have fought tirelessly against this from happening.

In the book, *State Budget Reform Toolkit*, written and published by American Legislative Exchange Council, the authors discuss the benefits of using both a spending limit and a rainy day fund is to help smooth out expenditures over the business cycle and avoid the danger of being forced to choose between core functions of government when revenues are less than expected. The purpose of the spending limit is to provide the fiscal discipline necessary during strong periods of revenue growth, to not over extend the budget by adding spending programs just because the state has additional revenues thereby creating a future structural deficit caused by unnecessary overspending.[12]

This two-pronged policy would make state budgets more resilient in the face of unanticipated emergency expenses and reduction in revenues due to a regional or national recession. For example, in Texas the Texas Windstorm Insurance Association is underfunded and therefore, will probably not have sufficient funds to pay all the possible claims that might be filed if a hurricane should hit the Texas coast. If this should occur, due to the inaccessibility of emergency funds the citizens of Texas would be subject to an immediate tax increase, or significant number of state employees would be laid off, or painful cuts in core government services would take place. None of these outcomes are choices we would want to make.

"It's time we reduced the federal budget and left the family budget alone."—Ronald Reagan

Adding New Tools To The Budget Process

The next step towards transforming your state government is for states to put every single budget item on the table for consideration. This means that many of the so called "holy grail" programs including entitlement programs are subject to review, change, and possible elimination. Only by allowing everything to be properly evaluated will state government be transformed. Legislators must stay focused on delivering effective services to taxpayers instead of spending money on ineffective social programs.

The days of taxing everything that moves or funding every project that feels good are gone forever. Taxpayers are demanding more efficiency and more accountability from their elected leaders. I believe it's time for real change in government, but you must be the change maker.

Below are some of the most expensive cost categories in a state budget. If spending is to be reduced these items must be seriously looked at with an open mind and when applying priority based budgeting standards.

- State Employees
- State Pensions
- State Retiree Health Care Plans
- State Medicaid Program

Reduce State Staffing By 10%

I can tell you from personal experience that during the 2011 Texas budget crisis I encountered a large degree of pushback by all of the state agency directors when I mentioned the idea of the possibility to reduce their staffing levels or FTE's (Full-Time Equivalents). Each of the directors argued for their need to retain every one of their current employees. In fact, many agency directors also attempted to justify their need to increase their staff levels. It is with this mentality that state government budgets have grown so much for the past 20 years.

If during the budget process there is a mention of staff reductions, those who support the idea of big government will speak against the idea of reducing staffing levels. If we add the influence of labor unions and other special interests then what you will get is a well-organized and a very vocal campaign that will flood the state capitol with hired protesters, and concern citizens that will demand that the state legislators not layoff any employees for any reason. During this time each legislator's office will be flooded with emails and faxes and much of this communication will contain accusations of racism.

These actions should not hinder your pursuit to have good government. It is up to Game Changers like you to stand up and be heard. We have all heard the saying, "When the going gets tough the tough get going." This principle is very true in politics.

To be heard by your legislators your voices must be as louder than those who wish to continue to grow government and who refuse to see the reality of the fiscal crisis. If you fail to show up in large numbers you have no one to blame but yourselves if the big government supporters persuade legislators to not reduce employee levels or if more spending is approved for more failed social programs.

In all my years of working for the State of Texas and Nueces County I am convinced that every single government entity, regardless of the type, has more employees than what are truly necessary. But, don't take my word on this. The proof is in the facts.

In 2008, the Thomas Jefferson Institute and Reason Foundation found that the state of Virginia had more than 7,600 non-critical positions (i.e., not public-safety, university faculty, and management-related positions) budgeted in their state budget. The report also stated that if Virginia would eliminate these positions it would save the state of Virginia over $500 million a year or more than $1 billion during the two-year budget. This is cost savings from only the non-critical positions.[13] Imagine the cost savings once you factor in the elimination of positions due to making the agency more efficient. This could easily translate into billions of dollars of savings.

Reform State Pensions

In recent years, state governments have encountered a funding crisis in their pension plans for public employees. According to a study conducted by the Pew Center on the States and released in June, 2012, states are $1.38 trillion in the hole when it comes to their pension and retiree health obligations. This means the American people are on the hook for this shortage. The report covers fiscal year 2010, which began July 1, 2009 in most states.[14]

Pew rated 11 states as "solid performers" in managing their pension obligations in fiscal year 2010—overall, these states were 90 percent funded. Two states—Texas and Wyoming—are new to this list since Pew began rating states in 2008. Wyoming improved its funding status, while Texas found ways to contribute more toward its pension bill from 2008 to 2010.[14]

However, for many other states due to the many years of underfunding a large number of states now face a $757 billion gap in their pension accounts. This means that states are now faced with three viable outcomes: (1) reduce program benefits; (2) taxpayers will have to make up this shortfall from future revenues or higher taxes; and (3) the stock market and other investments vehicles produce higher net returns than expected. In other words, the pension system gambles that the returns will be higher. Of these three options which one is more appealing? Common sense tells us none of these options are good.

The truth tells us it does not have to be this way, but rather legislators should take a pro-active approach towards solving this issue. It is far better to manage and minimize the discomfort change of this type may cause in comparison to the financial pain that will be caused at some point down the road. The problem we see in many state legislatures is that most legislators do not have the political courage to reduce the cost of government. They find it easier to place the burden and risk upon future generations of citizens.

Another very important fact to understand is this: Regardless of the type of pension plan that is in place, as long as these plans have a significant portion of the money invested in the stock market, they plans are fully exposed to all kinds of risk. In other words, most plans are fundamentally flawed. They are structurally designed to fail by design sooner or later. This is potentially a financial disaster looming on the horizon. There are other reasons or factors that will or may contribute to a serious fiscal crisis. These include:

- Escalation in health care costs
- Significant losses in the stock market
- Costly pension and health benefits provided in defined-benefit plans
- Public employees retiring earlier and living longer
- Reduction and postponement of employer contributions to the pension plans[15]

Using more realistic assumptions regarding the rate of return on assets, as well as assumptions regarding the actuarial value of liabilities, it's highly unlikely that these plans will achieve actuarial balance over the amortization period. Furthermore, pension systems are likely to experience significant funding shortfalls in future years, even if the economy recovers and financial markets stabilize. These funding shortfalls will impose a heavy burden on future generations and future budgets. This is not good for our children or for the economic health of our country or state.

Currently, the Texas' public pension systems are in relatively good standing; but these are extraordinary times and we must remain vigilant to ensure these systems' sustainability, a must for both taxpayers and beneficiaries.[16]

The truth is that it makes common and financial sense to not wait for the crisis to hit us, rather we could be pro-active and implement sensible, but fair, pension reform for all new enrollees and I want to emphasize, new employees. Now, there are the critics that will tell you that this kind of reform will not guarantee the solvency of the pension plans. That is true, expect for instead of the taxpayers being on the hook for the problems that may occur that risk is now transferred to the individual employees who is participating in the pension program. I cannot find anything in the U.S. Constitution that says the government or private industry should guarantee a retirement pension plan for employees and take on all the risk.

New Jersey Case Study

A good example of a person who fought the tidal wave of opponents and won is New Jersey Governor Chris Christie. Since he was elected in 2009, his budget proposals have included spending and tax cuts. In his budget proposal of 2011, Christie, who has gained a national reputation for coming down hard on public employees, asked public service employees to pay more for their health care. By raising their co-payments and premiums the state will save $323 million. By 2014, the governor's plan would require them to pay for 30% of their medical benefits, up from 8% now.[17]

Without serious pension reforms state legislatures will not be able to solve their long-term fiscal problems. It's not complicated. It's just simple math. Yet, there will always be serious push back by labor unions and other special interest groups when efforts are attempted to reform a state's pension program. Don't let this stop you from your goals of establishing polices that you believe lead to good government.

The truth is this is the only way to keep the pension system solvent for future generations of employees and more importantly transfer the risk to the employee rather than requiring future generations of taxpayers to be burdened with that risk. Most taxpayers do not have this kind of guarantee in their private sector jobs.

Utah Case Study

Utah also provides an excellent case study in what many people say was a successful state pension reform effort. In 2011, the Utah Legislature Utah switched from defined benefit to defined contribution pension for its public employees. Before I discuss the Utah plan I wish to explain the difference between a defined benefit plan and a defined contribution plan.[18]

A defined benefit plan is a specific type of retirement plan that most state employees have throughout America. A defined benefit plan specifies the amount of monthly benefits a qualifying employee will receive upon retirement. Investments made by the pension fund are assumed to be able to keep up with the amount owed, even though this clearly has not happened in reality in most state pension plans.

By contrast, a defined contribution plan specifies how much the employee and employer will contribute. The amount of future benefits is not guaranteed. However, employees control their own plan, can invest it however they want, can take it with them if they leave, and crucially perhaps, the state cannot attempt to loot it to pay for current obligations.

Under the Utah plan, all new hires have a defined contribution plan with the state contributing a generous 10% of pay. They can also choose a defined benefit plan, but the state contribution remains the same at 10% and is not open-ended. This guarantees that Utah knows precisely how much it will have to pay. Even a stock market crash can't force them to pay more. Most other state legislatures are legally obligated to fund their state pension plan's shortfall. This means that shortfall must be made up with your tax dollars.[18]

This kind of reform benefits all the stakeholders: taxpayers, public employees, and government. Workers own their retirement account and can carry it to another job. Government benefits because politicians are no longer forced to divert funds that are needed in other areas of the budget to have to pay for pension plan obligations. As for taxpayers they benefit by no longer having to bear the risk of having to pay higher taxes to cover the loss of plan values if the stock market declines.[18]

Since the implementation of Utah's new plan there have been many people criticizing the rate of returns and the structure of the plan citing that the government's better suited to manage pension plans to ensure their solvency. Well, once again let me state a fact:

it is not government's basic core function to do this kind of thing. Government's primary job is to protect the citizens and promote the opportunity to pursue happiness. Perhaps when the next financial depression hits or serious recession Texas and many other states should seriously consider adopting a pension plan like Utah's.

Restructure State Retiree Health Care Plans

According to the Center for State and Local Government Excellence, financing health care benefits for state employees at their current benefit levels is fiscally unsustainable. Recent estimates suggest that the states have $627 billion in unfunded retiree health care liabilities for current and future benefits, according to the Center for State and Local Government Excellence. States have not done nearly enough to set aside money for their retirees' health care and other non-pension benefits such as life insurance. As of fiscal year 2010, they had put away only 5 percent of their total bill coming due for those benefits.[14]

For example, according to the Texas Public Policy Foundation, a non-partisan Austin based think tank, the cost of providing health insurance to Texas' state employees and retirees has increased about $2 billion, 94 percent since the 2000-01 biennium.[19]

Currently, Texas pays for 100 percent of health insurance premiums for state employees. The total number of state employees is estimated to be 235,047 in 2013 which is an increase of more than 16,700 employees since 2006. State contributions to employee and retiree group health insurance for 2012-13 will be $4.1 billion, or 2.4 percent of the state budget. This is a $1.5 billion increase from 2000-01, representing an average biennial increase of more than 20 percent. Under the current benefit program the state's contributions will continue to grow. The solution to the long term problem is either change the program to reduce the cost to the state or increase revenues through economic expansion so to avoid having to raise taxes.[19]

Additionally, those employees who share in the cost of dependent coverage have seen their monthly cost rise every year. In both cases, costs are increasing without any corresponding increase in real benefits. Both employees and taxpayers suffer. This results in a larger percentage of the state's budget putting additional pressure on the state budget during a time when revenues are not sufficient to support additional costs.

All over America taxpayers are no longer willing to bear the increasing cost of these plans in the form of higher employer contribution rates or decreased government services. They are demanding reforms that will lower their costs plus they are willing to accept a change in plan benefits if necessary. State government experts say that states will not be able to sustain the state's health care commitments to retirees unless the system is restructured. Without these necessary reforms, states will continue to financially struggle resulting in less funding for things such as education, health care, or public safety.

One idea that have been proposed is to phase in, over the next four to six years, a 30% increase in employee contributions to the cost of the monthly premium for employee only and increase the cost to employees for family coverage to 75% from the current 50%. Another idea is to offer state employees the option of a high deductible health plan and Health Savings Account (HSA) to control cost and allow employees to share in the premium savings. State employees should have the choice of enrolling in a high deductible health plan with the minimum high deductible allowed under law and a plan with an even higher deductible, in order to give state employees the most choice. Unfortunately, none of these ideas have been passed out of committee.[20] Now I have to ask this question, "Why not?" Perhaps it's because many legislators believe that the budget dollars they discuss actually "belong to them" rather than to the taxpayers.

According to the Texas Public Policy Foundation, the savings to the state from HSAs would also decrease the unfunded liability for retirement benefits, which was estimated by the Texas Pension

Review Board to be $38.5 billion as of February 2010 in Texas. Switching to HSAs could improve the viability of the program in future years and at the least would give legislators more flexibility in meeting the other obligations of the state.[20]

Once again I wish to state that there is not requirement by either the U.S. or the Texas Constitution that requires that taxpayers assume the financial risk and burden for employee benefit programs. The real issue that whether or not future generations of Texans will be financially responsible to pay for a benefit they possibly will not have for themselves. The fact remains that Texas, as well as all the other states must take action to rethink and reform these kinds of employee benefit plans.

Reform State Medicaid Program

In a recent publication titled, *The Big Squeeze,* issued by the Texas Public Policy Foundation, authored by Arlene Wohlgemuth & Spencer Harris, they write, "Medicaid's growth rate is simply unsustainable. The program threatens to bankrupt the state. Even without the PPACA, Medicaid costs will double every 10 years, growing to $38.3 billion in the 2020-21 biennium; $72.5 billion in 2030-31; and $144.5 billion in 2040-41. To continue the program as currently structured, the state must immediately raise taxes or cut other programs to make room for Medicaid's growth. Neither of these alternatives is acceptable."[21]

This leaves little doubt as to whether future generations of the poor will have access to affordable health care. Another well-known fact is that legislative incremental policy changes are not sufficient to address this massive fiscal problem that has plagued states for the past 15 years.

Therefore, it is vital that in your pursuit of good government policies to transform your state government, you should include the need to address the issue of the ever increasing Medicaid costs in your state. Because they are not just health insurance and health care issues; they represent a fiscal crisis that threatens the entire Texas state budget, limiting the funds available to other programs, such as education and public safety.

The inherent structure of Medicaid encourages states to spend more and more money on providing care, but the small incremental attempts to limit costs do not resolve the fundamental problem of Medicaid spending. Medicaid as an entitlement program that encourages overspending and poor health decisions by enrollees because there is no financial link between the care received and the person receiving the care. The time for action is now, not later.

Thus, it is vital that states such as Texas begin immediately to reform the state's Medicaid program for the better. However, these reforms must be carefully designed to ensure against recreating the same problems such as rising caseload and mandated benefits that have plagued Medicaid since its inception.

For example, in a report issued by the Texas Policy Foundation titled, *Medicaid Reform,* the authors talk about the alternative program that was implemented in 2008, in the state of Rhode Island. The state received $12 billion federal Medicaid dollars spread out over five years to pay the federal portion of the state's Medicaid costs. Rhode Island still spends up front the equivalent amount of state dollars that it would under the Federal Medical Assistance Percentage rates but with more flexibility to spend the money on custom programs. These are not customarily permitted under Medicaid rules.[22]

States must search for ways to reduce the burden of Medicaid on their budgets. States should look to the successes and lessons learned from other states' experiments in structuring and implementing an alternative to the Medicaid structure. Among these showing success are Rhode Island's Global Medicaid Waiver, Indiana's Healthy Indiana Plan, Florida's Cash & Counseling program, and University Health System's CareLink program in San Antonio.[22]

So far under this new system of delivery of services, Rhode Island has not cut services, run out of money, or dropped people from enrollment. The Rhode Island plan pays for community care and home health care in preference to nursing home care. Already the state has spent less money than anticipated under the plan. Of the $2.6 billion planned in the first year of the waiver, only $1.7 billion was actually allocated and spent. Flexibility and lack of federal strings attached to the money are the factors generally credited for the savings.[22]

Based on those states that have led the way for finding workable Medicaid reform plans, it seems clear that by allowing the free market to control health care spending after financial links are established the overall demand for health care without threatening the health of individuals greatly reduced as well as the cost for receiving those services. It seems that the main reason for these results is because individuals now are personally responsible for managing their own healthcare. The bottom line is that replacing our current system of how we administer and deliver Medicaid paid services is not a choice but a necessity.

To deal effectively in this area state legislators should consider rising Medicaid costs not just health insurance and health care issues for the poor, but they must see this expenditure for what it truly represents: a fiscal crisis that threatens hard working families and the entire Texas state budget by limiting the funds available to other programs, such as education and public safety.

The inherent structure of Medicaid encourages states to view Medicaid spending as an entitlement program, the holy grail of politics. Legislators know that if they vote to change it they will have to answer to the people of Election Day and therefore, many of our legislators don't want to do what really needs to be done. Until legislators have the political courage to require Medicaid enrollees to be personally responsible for how they use this benefit, the program will continue to see overspending and poor health decisions by enrollees because they have vested interest in their decisions or as some refer to as they "no skin in the game."

Proven Strategies to Create Jobs

"Texas is a state where a dream can be put to work."—Rick Perry

Time and again we have learned that the best way to achieve growth and create jobs is for hardworking people to keep more of their own money in their own pockets."—Chris Chocola

Adopt Policies That Create Jobs

During a visit to Washington D.C. where I was attending the first ever GOPAC Emerging Leaders Conference, I was asked many times by Representatives and Senators from all over the country what Texas was doing to lead the nation in job creation. The simple answer I gave them was: That just how we do things in Texas. But the actual answer isn't that simple. The truth is that our ability to lead the nation in job creation took many years of doing the right things legislatively. Among which included our conservative approach to preparing our state budgets and willingness to adopt some much needed tort laws which help stabilize some of the risk in the business community.

This all began 1994 when George W. Bush become the Governor of Texas and he was followed by Governor Rick Perry. These men set the tone for the Texas Legislature to adopt and implement many key pieces of legislation that created a friendly, predicable, pro-business environment in Texas. These key pieces of legislation established the foundation which is largely responsible for creating thousands of private sector jobs Texas has experienced over the past 10 years.

The fundamental principle that was used to write into law these key components of job creation was the purposeful intent of the Governor and the Texas Legislature to limit government's role in our economic environment. Bill Peacock, Vice President of Research and Planning and Director, Center for Economic Freedom, in a published report titled, *Texas' Economic Leadership Due to Our Leadership in Limited Government Policies,* said, "Since June 2009, when the recession ended, Texas has added 265,300 new jobs, accounting for 45 percent of net U.S. job creation. Over the last ten years, the numbers are even better: Texas created more than 1 million jobs during this period, more than all other states combined; while California, New York, Florida, and Illinois have combined lost 930,000 jobs."[23]

The question we all should be asking ourselves, especially if we want to transform our state government into a more effective and efficient government is "Why?" The answer lies in what businesses are looking for to setup operations. One of the biggest factors that come into the decision making process is the matter of taxation. Consider this: Texas ranks 50th among the states in state tax burden, compared with California at 9, New York at 11, Florida at 36, and Illinois at 25. When given a choice to pay low taxes or higher taxes the business owners always pick lower taxes.[23]

The economic success that the state of Texas has generated during these past 10 years is referred to by the media and economists as "Texas model." This model is predominately built upon free market principles. The free market seeks to bring and keep businesses in a state by providing the best economic climate for people to live, work, and do business. It keeps taxes low, provide for a predictable legal environment, keeps regulations at a minimum, and generally tries to keep government out of people's lives. What we have done in Texas is to follow some fundamental, time proven principles that actually work in creating jobs.

By doing these five things very well in Texas we are able to attract and retain the best employers in the world. But, don't take our word, just look at what others are saying about Texas:

- Area Development: "Texas Wins 2013 Gold Shovel Award"—05/2913
- Chief Executive Magazine: "Texas Best State for Business for 9th Year in a Row"—05/07/13
- Site Selection: "Texas Wins the 2012 Governor's Cup"—03/04/13
- Chief Executive Magazine: "Texas Best State for Business for 8th Year in a Row"—05/21/12
- FDI Magazine: Governor's Award 2012, 08/20/12
- Forbes: "In Case You Missed It: Texas Cities Dominate Forbes' Rankings of Best Cities for Jobs"—05/12/11
- Chief Executive Magazine: "Texas Best State for Business for Seventh Consecutive Year"—05/04/11
- Site Selection: 'Texas Wins the 2010 Governor's Cup'—03/02/11
- Texas Ranked Top Exporting State for 9th Consecutive Year—02/16/11
- Newsweek: 'For Sheer Economic Promise, No Place Beats Texas'—11/15/10
- SIRVA: 'No. 1 relocation destination in the U.S. for six-straight years'—01/10/11
- CNBC: 'America's Top State for Business'—July, 2010
- Chief Executive Magazine: 'For the sixth year in a row, CEOs rated Texas as the #1 state for Business'—May, 2010
- Wiser Trade: 'No. 1 exporting U.S. state for eight straight years'—February, 2010
- 'Kiplinger: Texas dominates Kiplinger's Cities with the Lowest Cost of Living list in 2011'—June, 2011

If you want our state government to generate thousands of new jobs, then you must lobby your legislators to implement the principles incorporated in the Texas model. A state that keeps its taxes low and overregulation at bay is one that fosters economic development. On the other hand, a state that plows its cash into government spending is one whose businesses and citizens will soon be leaving for greener pastures. Just take a look at what is happening in California, Illinois, and Ohio to name a few states that are losing thousands of jobs each year.

Let me summarize the five things we have done in Texas to achieve a terrific pro-business environment.

- Established a state funded economic incentive program
- Keep taxes low
- Strive for reasonable regulations
- Implemented a fair and predictable legal system
- Reward job creators

Now let's take a closer look at each of these pro-business activities.

Create State Funded Economic Incentive Programs

At Governor Rick Perry's request, the Texas legislature created the Texas Enterprise Fund (TEF) in 2003 and since then has re-appropriated funding to help ensure the growth of Texas businesses and create more jobs throughout the state. TEF projects must be approved by the governor, lieutenant governor and speaker of the House. The fund has since become one of the state's most competitive tools to recruit and bolster business. To date, the TEF has invested more than $397 million and closed the deal on projects generating more than 53,600 new jobs and more than $14.4 billion in capital investment in the state.[24]

Another effective program used by Texas to create jobs is the Industry Cluster Initiative. On October 20, 2004 Governor Rick Perry announced his vision for building the future economy of the state of Texas by focusing on building competitive advantages through six target industry clusters. As a result of this vision the Texas Emerging Technology Fund (TETF) was created by the Texas Legislature in 2005 at the urging of Gov. Perry to provide Texas with an unparalleled advantage in the research, development, and commercialization of emerging technologies. TETF grants are awarded in the following three areas:

- Research Superiority Acquisition—funds for Texas higher education institutions to recruit the best research talent in the world.
- Commercialization Awards—funds to help companies take ideas from concept to development to ready for the marketplace.
- Matching Awards—funds create public-private partnerships which leverage the unique strengths of universities, federal government grant programs, and industry. [24]

The TETF brings new ideas and products to the marketplace today. This innovation and the commercialization will have a profound long-term impact on Texas. Priority is given to emerging technology projects that will enhance our state's global competitiveness. Not only will these TETF investments demonstrate economic benefits but also result in significant medical and or scientific breakthroughs which will improve people's lives.

To date, the TETF has allocated more than $197 million in funds to 133 early-stage companies, and nearly $173 million in grant matching and research superiority funds to Texas universities. Since the inception of the TETF, over $407 million in additional investment from other sources following on to the TETF investment have come to these Texas companies. That means that TETF funds have been more than doubled by other non-state sources, providing much needed funding for small, innovative companies in difficult financial times.[25]

However, since the creation of the Texas Enterprise Fund and the Texas Emerging Technology Fund have both come under heavy criticism from their opponents. Several watchdog organizations have argued for years that both Funds are nothing more than a slush fund that allows Governor Rick Perry to reward allies and political donors. Another criticism is that the fund has not been audited either by the Texas State Auditor's Office or by an independent auditing firm since 2003.[26] This obvious lack of transparency is very troubling for the governor's office since Texas has been making national news because of the Comptroller's enacted programs to increase government transparency throughout Texas government entities.

I firmly believe that these two fund programs should not be handled in the manner that is currently being used. Rather, I believe the Governor should select an independent board that is made up of volunteers form a wide range of industries in Texas as well as private citizens. The board should include the Governor, Lt. Governor, Comptroller, and the House Speaker in addition to the board members. Plus, one of the first actions the board should take is the approval of an independent auditing firm that will be responsible to conduct an annual audit of both funds. The audit report is then to be released to the members of the Texas Legislature.

Low Taxes Means More Jobs

In July, 2012, CNBC compiled its 2012 Best States for Business index, using factors ranging from business friendliness to quality of life to determine which states are the best places for entrepreneurs to set up shop. With little surprise, Texas led the way as the best overall state for business, a product of its business-friendly tax environment and a relatively low cost of living. CNBC was particularly impressed with its overall economy, including diversity of businesses, earning the overall number one for that category in particular.[27]

In the published report titled, *Competitive States 2010: Texas vs. California,* the authors stated that Texas' economic strength lies in its ability to create jobs.[26] According to employment data released by the Bureau of Labor Statistics, Texas created 129,000 new jobs in 2009—over one-half of all the new jobs in the U.S. In contrast, California lost 112,000 jobs during the same period. Texas continues to do a fine job of adding to its employment numbers. Since June 2009, which marked the official end of the recession, until July 2011, the number of jobs increased in the state by 328,000.[27]

Therefore, why is it that Texas has such a significant competitive advantage over states like California? The answers are simple:

1. Texas has no income tax where most states like California have a steeply progressive income tax.
2. Texas' appropriate level of government spending relative to the income of working Texans keeps its economy strong.
3. Texas has a predictable and lighter regulatory burden which helps its economy flourish in comparison to other states like California.

Mr. Laffer states, "Our study shows that it is these Texas policies of relatively low taxes, low spending, and less regulation that have helped the Lone Star State weather the Great Recession better than California and the nation as a whole." There you have it. The Texas model works not just in Texas, but these principles can work anywhere in the world.[28]

The facts are strong. Consider what a senior economist at the Federal Reserve Bank in Dallas had to say about Texas' growth: "Since the severe oil-shock recession and banking crisis of the mid-1980s, Texas economic growth has consistently exceeded that of the nation. Jobs were added at a faster annual rate in Texas than in the U.S. in all but two years since 1990."[28]

On average, Texas jobs have grown at about 2% annually over the past 20 years compared with about 1% for the U.S. Significantly, the rapid employment increase did not come at the expense of income growth. Real Gross Domestic Product (GDP) per capita expansion of about 1.5% per year kept pace with the nation during this period.[29]

However, all good things are not guaranteed to continue as they are. In order to keep an economy going in the right direction, Texas could be passed by other states if it simply relies on its past record. Consider for a moment the huge $25 billion budget shortfall the Texas Legislature in 2011. This provided a great opportunity for Texas to reassert its commitment to low taxes, pro-business, predictable legal, and regulatory environments.

For the third time in 20 years, Texas faced the challenge to once again increase spending because of outcries from the public, or to find common sense solutions to balance the budget without raising taxes while prioritizing its major spending needs. The Texas Legislature did what was right, rather than what was popular. In the 2011Texas Legislative Session the Texas Legislature avoided California's path toward overspending and economic decline, by reducing total state spending by $15 billion from the previous state budget, and thereby, maintaining its strong commitment to reduce government spending.

Yet, in two short years the lessons from the past were all forgotten. During the 2013 Texas Legislature made history by approving the largest spending budget in Texas history. When the State Comptroller certified $102 billion for spending the Texas Legislature forgot its conservative fiscal policy values and spent all they money they could get their hands on.

Watching the budget play out over the years I have learned that the media loves to report news in ways that exceed the public's interest. In both budget years 2003 and 2011 when Texas faced a $10 billion and $25 billion shortfall, many people, including most of the media, criticized the work of the Texas Legislature when the budget failed to increase taxes and the Legislature chose to cut spending to balance the budget. The media and Democrats cried, "Foul" and made all kind s of disturbing assertions that the budget cuts would end up in a catastrophic end of days as we know them. Yet, the truth is that none of their claims came true. By showing fiscal restraint during a budget shortfall the Texas Legislature proved that common sense and financial restraints work whether you do it on a kitchen table or in the Texas Legislature.

Facts are stubborn things and the fact is that when state government embraces and legislates with intent to provide a business environment that has relatively low taxes, low government spending, and fewer regulations these decisions will lead to higher economic growth in good times and lower declines in bad times.

Should Texas be a model for America? In many ways absolutely, but there will always be those naysayers and some commentators, who will be quick to jump all over Texas' flaws, at the first moment of trouble. I say let them talk all they want.

I want you to know that when state government chooses to adopt and implement proven, conservative fiscal policy it works every time it is used. History provides us the evidence to back up this claim. When state government believes in restoring individual and economic freedom for all its citizens the people prosper. When state government chooses to provide the private sector economic incentives the people prospers with an infusion of new jobs and the government benefits with an increase in tax revenue. This represents a true win-win scenario.

When state government is willing to spend only what the government has available then and prioritize its spending then the people prosper. Legislatures from other states would do well to look at what we have done in Texas as a model of governance worthy to duplicate. The data from Texas is just too compelling to ignore the facts. However, there is always a trade off in financial matters. The accounting term for this trade-off is called "the opportunity costs." I will speak more about this later.

The stakes are high. The global economy forces us to complete with our neighboring states as well as with every other country in the world for jobs and a strong robust economy. If state legislators are going to be successful, they first will have to take the process of getting big things done in state government very seriously. They must implement innovative and competitive legislation in order to change the way the state does business.

Eliminate Waste And Unnecessary Regulations

In 1982, President Ronald Reagan said, "We're from the government, and we're here to help!" Since that time, we have grown accustom to hearing stories about the inadequacies and inability of our government, regardless of its level, to be able to accomplish any task efficient and effectively. Today, more than ever in our nation's history every level of government is too big and spends too much money on things it should not be spending money on. Lean Six Sigma expert, Michael George, estimates that the budget of the average government entity (federal, state, county or city) contains approximately 25% of wasteful spending woven into the budget. In other words, if the state budget is $100 billion, there is an estimated $25 billion in wasteful spending in the budget.

Shortly after the Texas Legislature ended its Special Session on June 30, 2011, I had the opportunity to visit with Mark Escamilla, Del Mar College President, regarding the impact the budget cuts was having on the college. He told me that due to the reduced funding in their budget he chose to outsource their janitorial services to a private local company. He said the annual savings from the decision was going to be nearly $700,000. Similar results were achieved at Texas A&M University-Corpus Christi for outsourcing their janitor services. This pattern is not just a coincidence. In most cases all across America it is more costly for government to do something that needs to be done than it does for private sector to do that very same task.

Dr. Arthur B. Laffer, he concludes his report by saying,

> "Whether you focus on theory or history, or the federal level versus the state level, the lesson is clear: government intervention in the marketplace wastes resources, harms consumers, and often achieves the opposite from its intended goal. A deregulated and lightly taxed market is the best vehicle to achieve prosperity and a good life for all citizens."[30]

In 1996, the U.S. Congress commissioned a committee to study the effects of federal regulations on the nation's economy. The final report was titled, *Smothering Economic Growth One Regulation at a Time.*"[31]

The United States has gone from an economic backwater of a few relatively small colonies to the largest, most prosperous economy in the world. Through much of the post-World War II period, the United States economy has been the envy of the world. However, our recent economic history has been disappointing. The current expansion has been hampered by high taxes and regulation. In 1995, Congress released two Joint Economic Committee (JEC) studies that revealed that excessive government is harmful to economic growth and worker's incomes. Serious economic reform must reduce the size and scope of the federal government.[31]

Of particular concern to many entrepreneurs is the federal regulatory burden. In a recent poll, fifty-two percent of mid-sized firms said that government regulation was their biggest concern. They were more concerned about regulations than about making a profit, paying taxes, or controlling health-care costs. Clearly, reducing the regulatory burden is vital to create the basis for robust economic growth.

Economic Growth and Regulation

Regulations work like taxes. It makes no difference to the entrepreneur, or the economy, whether the entrepreneur must write a $10,000 check to the government for taxes or a $10,000 check to comply with a regulation. Forcing the entrepreneur to comply with regulations that harms economic development by diverting resources to less-productive uses is another example of government wasteful spending.

Economic growth is created by entrepreneurs efficiently providing goods and services to their consumers. Regulations interfere with the basic process of production. Unfortunately for the American taxpayers, too many of our country's elected leaders know nothing about creating jobs. In fact, some of our legislators, like our current President, have never owned a business. Furthermore, the economic well-being of consumers is maximized by satisfying their wants at the lowest possible costs. Regulations raise costs just like taxes and hinder entrepreneurs from investing in their business either through asset acquisition or capital investments. Higher business costs of any kind slows economic growth which in turn results in reduced incomes and possibly leads to more dependent upon some form of government program.

Small Business and Regulation

The public perception of government regulations is that all the regulations provide some kind of tremendous public good. For example, the regulation that drivers be licensed to drive. While on the surface that is a very good idea, the fact of the matter is that it has not stopped bad drivers from driving a car and harming other people due to their careless or irresponsible driving. Regardless of the good intentions that a particular regulation may proposed to have the fact is that the costs of federal and state regulations are enormous.

Other fact we must all know is that the government's reach into our lives extends well beyond Washington's taxes, deficits, and borrowing. For the first time in the 20 years that the institute has been attempting to measure the cost of government agencies' regulations that cost now the cost of federal regulations exceeds half of the annual budget, at $1.8 trillion. When added to the budget itself, which is rapidly approaching $4 trillion a year, government is absorbing more than a third of the nation's economic output either directly or indirectly. In other words, it harms our economy more than it helps.[32]

Today, hardworking families like yours and mine "pay" nearly $15,000 a year in hidden regulatory taxes. Small businesses, regulations cost almost $11,000 per employee. And the trend is ever upward. In the past 20 years, more than 81,000 rules have been issued, more than 3,500 a year, or more than nine every day. That works out to about 30 new rules issued by agencies for every law passed by Congress. And there are another 4,000 proposed rules in the pipeline the cost of which CEI can't yet measure.[33]

The federal government lists all of its regulations in the *Code of Federal Regulations*. It is more than 169,000 pages long and growing. Last year alone, 3,807 new final rules were published in the Federal Register—more than 10 per day. In 2010, it was 3,573 new rules.[34]

Regulation is also damaging to innovation. The purpose of federal regulation is to change economic behavior in ways Washington bureaucrats think are appropriate. However, the very nature of innovation is its unpredictability. Environmental regulation traditionally identified methods whereby industries were to achieve pollution reduction. In one instance, industries were forced to install expensive smoke scrubbers to remove sulphur from plant exhaust. However, there were cheaper methods to achieve the same outcome. The reason for the language of regulation often has little to do with improving safety or economic well-being. It is to reward a favored constituency.[31]

To cite one example among hundreds of cost and interference with innovation consider the case of Amoco's Yorktown, Virginia, refinery. In 1997, the Environmental Protection Agency directed Amoco Corporation to spend $31 million to remove benzene from its wastewater in its treatment plant. Amoco showed that it could remove four times as much benzene from its wastewater in other areas of the plant for only $6 million. Clearly, it would be better for the health of the community to reduce more benzene. Amoco's argument was that the interests of the community lie in lower levels of benzene. However, the interests of the regulators were to have the company comply with the mandated regulations. Regulators too often follow the book rather than look at the interests of the community. If Amoco were allowed to flexibly meet environmental goals, they could have saved $25 million while improving the health of the community.[35]

The productive economy is an economy with minimal regulation. The Joint Economic Committee (JEC) has issued many reports highlighting the direct and indirect cost of big government. The stagnation of family incomes under Clinton are the direct result of his Administration's failure to curb the size and scope of the Federal government.[35] If we are concerned with the inadequate rate of economic growth, we must recognize that the single greatest impediment to economic growth is the size and scope of the Federal government. Unless we can reduce the extent of regulation and introduce some economic rationality to important regulations, we cannot hope to see incomes rise to provide a better future for our children and future generations.

Just as our Texas Legislature is supposed to pass a budget every two years for what it spends, it should pass a regulatory budget. If it caps regulatory burdens at, say, $10 billion, it would then have to prioritize which rules it believes provide the most bang for the buck. Voters would also know when the Legislature votes to increase regulatory costs, giving members at least some incentive to keep regulation in check.

The fight for real regulatory reform is one that has not been fought on the front lines and that is because "We the People" have been kept in the dark about it and because most politicians have shown a lack of leadership to tackle this cost and intrusive form of government. Well, those days are behind us now. The only way this win is to fight. That is why politicians and agencies are so resistant to reforms like a regulatory budget. This kind of transparency opens the eyes of the people and if enough people learn the truth about regulatory costs, the politicians lose.

Fair and Predictable Legal System

History has a way to teach us many lessons. One of those lessons is that if there is little or no tort reform in a state, there will be low economic growth and high unemployment.

Case Study

The state of Texas is a perfect example of this truth. Prior to enacting tort reform in 1995, Texas' economy was struggling along like most states. Texas civil courts were a national laughingstock, known to be notoriously unfair and a huge deterrent to businesses that wanted to grow and expand. The Wall Street Journal called Texas the "lawsuit capital of the world" and 60 Minutes produced a segment entitled, "Justice for Sale" in Texas. Lloyds of London imposed an insurance surcharge on any company that did business in Texas because of the high probability and excessive cost of lawsuits.[36]

In 1995 the Texas Legislature passed a series of bills to reform the state's civil justice system. These bills addressed: limits on punitive damages, joint and several liability, sanctions for filing frivolous suits, limits on venue shopping and out-of-state filings, modifications to deceptive trade practices and medical malpractice reform. This began a transformation in the way people viewed the Texas economy.

The work for tort reform did not stop here. In 2003, the Texas Legislature passed House Bill 4 which was a sweeping package of civil justice reforms that was to serve as model for other states. This bill provided for common sense package of long overdue civil justice reforms.

In 2011 Texas Legislature continued its goal of adding more tort reform related legislation with the passage of HB 274. The bill implements several measures to streamline and lower the cost of litigation in Texas courts, allowing parties to resolve disputes more quickly, more fairly and less expensively.[37]

Collectively these reforms have created an honest and predictable civil justice system in Texas. This civil justice system ensures timely compensation for legitimately injured parties and a fair determination of liability for those who are alleged to have caused harm to others.[37]

The Perryman Group's analysis shows that lawsuit reform has the additional benefit of nurturing the state's economic growth in a variety of ways, each producing a ripple effect throughout the Texas economy. Business owners and taxpayers save millions of dollars by eliminating non-productive expenditures related to unnecessary litigation, including administrative costs, court costs and the waste of the time of executives and workers.

The Perryman Group concludes that approximately 8.5% of Texas' economic growth since 1995 is the result of lawsuit reforms.[37] The economic gains attributable to these reforms include:

- **$112.5 billion** increase in annual spending
- **$51.2 billion** increase in annual output—goods and services produced in Texas
- **$2.6 billion** increase in annual state tax revenue
- **$468.9 million** in annual benefits from safer products
- **$15.2 billion** in annual net benefits of enhanced innovation
- **499,000** permanent jobs
- **430,000** additional Texans have health insurance today as a result of the medical liability reforms

The Consequences of Not Implementing Tort Reform

The research is undeniable. The economic consequences of such heavy tort costs are considerable. First, individuals suffer directly by having less disposable income than they would otherwise due to higher premium costs for insurance. Second, individuals suffer indirectly when businesses, forced to pay higher premiums for product liability and other forms of insurance, raise their prices on goods and services. Third, when businesses have to charge higher prices, they do less business than they would otherwise, which in turn slows down job expansion and economic growth.

Individuals incur the most harm with in the form of lower wages and fewer jobs when the economy slowdown. Finally, increasing litigiousness discourages businesses and individuals from taking risks, which means that fewer new products are brought to market and new technologies are either delayed or forgone altogether.

The Benefits of Tort Reform

Texas' economy continues to receive national and international recognition. Under Governor Perry's leadership, Texas has been the nation's job creation capital, creating approximately half of America's net jobs in the past two years alone, and more private sector jobs in the last 10 years than any other state. Additionally, according to a USA Today examination of data released by the Bureau of Economic Analysis, Texas moved past New York over the past decade to become the nation's second-largest economy.[38] According to the Bureau of Labor Statistics Texas' unemployment rate has also remained well below the national average, and for the period January, 2011 through November, 2013, Texas added over 632,000 jobs which was more than any other state.[39]

"The evidence is clear: Economic prosperity is attainable for those states that exercise discretion and discipline in spending and taxation. Pro-growth tax and fiscal policies—like those championed by ALEC and throughout Rich States, Poor States—set a clear path to a renewed national economic recovery."—Rick Perry

Making Government Excellent

"The private sector is motivated by profit and efficiency and the US government often is not."—Eric Anderson

"As Justice Brandeis noted, one of the happy aspects of the federal system is that a state may serve as a laboratory and try novel policy experiments. In 2012, the 'Texas Experiment' of light taxation and regulation produced more jobs than any state, and an economy growing at twice the national state average."—Ted Cruz

The Problems We Face in America Today

Never in the history of our nation have States been so challenged to get their financial houses in order. Nevertheless, I believe that these difficult days also present tremendous opportunities for state governments to fundamentally reform the state governments' structures, systems, and legislative agenda. Today's fiscal situation leaves them no choice. It is either transform the government structure or be left behind in the race to provide good plentiful jobs, economic opportunity for investments and a higher standard of living for its citizens.

In the book, *Rich States, Poor States 6th Edition*, Dr. Arthur B. Laffer, Stephen Moore, and Jonathan Williams provide invaluable insight into each of the 50 "laboratories of democracy." With solid empirical research and the latest data on state economies, the evidence is clear on which state tax and fiscal policies directly lead to more opportunities, more jobs, and more prosperity for all Americans.[40]

The answer is simple. For most states the government is broken. From the White House to the School House and everything in between, government is inefficient and very ineffective. For years the policy experts have taken the position that in order to solve today's complex problems we need big government and more money. Well history, once again has clearly proven that this approach to our nation's problems does not work and is immoral to burden future generations of Americans with debt that will create a severe financial hardship in the years to come.

Currently, we are at a crisis point in the United States. As of June, 2013 America has accumulated $17 trillion deficit and it continues to grow daily at approximately $4 billion per day. The public has low confidence in government. A recent CNN survey found that 86 percent of Americans feel that the federal government is broken.[41] So it isn't just me who believe this, it is also millions of other Americans. So the time to take action is now. You and I must get involved demand from our elected leaders that put America and our local and state government on a road to achieve financial soundness if we are to secure a robust and promising future for our country, state, and city.

We can and must start to change our country's economic course by providing an environment that rewards our citizens for their efforts and their risks. The founders of our country understood that a republic with its multiple states was the perfect incubator for testing competing approaches to public policies. States have a unique opportunity to fix what is broken. This is where you can have the biggest impact. By requesting and demanding that the new generation of political leaders listen to your voices, you can motivate them to adapt the new tools and proven fiscal policies that are necessary to win the battle for truly effective and efficient government.

Government Must Change

Let me be very clear on this point. We can't win the future with a government of the past, but unfortunately right now in many ways that's exactly what we have. We have a government of the past. Government has been acting, thinking, and solving problems like we did 60 years ago. As many of you know, the last major reorganization of the federal government took place during the Truman Administration mainly through the work of a commission led by former President Herbert Hoover.

Through these past 60 years changes to our government have generally been smaller and more targeted. We've seen departments created in response of the moment or to fulfill a campaign promise. We've seen big departments broken into smaller departments which over time have grown into big departments. Rarely have we seen departments or agencies downsize much less eliminated. And here is one of the major reasons why our government is broken.

During the past 70 years we have seen the rise of the internet, the wide use of the cell phone and tablet computer, the globalization of our markets, the explosion of our deficit, the aging of our population and the transformation of our national security from the Cold War to the War on Terror. We now live in the Information Age and our lives today are totally different from those of our grandparents.

However, despite all these dramatic shifts in how we live our lives, the government hasn't changed that much at all. We still have roughly the same overall formal structure that was designed over 60 ago. All we have managed to do is just added layers of new agencies and programs over the years. And no matter where you fall in the political spectrum, whether you consider yourself a Democrat, Republican, or Independent, we can all agree that our government is broken.

In the book, *Letting Go of the Status Quo, a Playbook for Transforming State Government*, the authors, agree that most states find themselves shackled by the old ways of governing. In addition, they state, A redesign is urgently needed because as state governments struggle to respond to the imperatives for change, many find themselves hampered by their dated practice programs, old style hierarchical organizations; obsolete pension systems; service models driven by bureaucracy instead of citizen needs; budgets that ignore results and transparency; and tax systems designed around yesterday's economy and technology."[42]

Consider for a moment the exorbitantly high costs embedded in our education system, which is still based on old business models and archaic laws. According to a report prepared by Deloitte Research titled, *Driving More Money into the Classroom: The Promise of Shared Services*, in many states, at least 40 cents of every dollar spent on schools never makes it into the classroom, in Texas it is 50 cents, and teachers make up a little more than half of all school district staff.[43]

One reason for this is because of the hundreds if not thousands of tiny school districts, each operating its own transportation, human resources, food services, information technology, building maintenance, administration and other support functions. The same kind of huge administrative inefficiencies can be observed in the duplication and overlap between many county and city governments and special districts in states across the country.

The problem here isn't just how the government is structured, but also has to do with how well it works. I am sure that most of us can agree that our government is filled with talented, dedicated public minded employees who want to serve the country for all the right reasons. But for too long many of their best efforts have been undermined by outdated systems and by outdated processes that waste taxpayer dollars and don't deliver measurable results. The truth is that the revolutions in technology and operations that have transformed the private sector haven't always found their way into government.

Because of this the opportunity for waste, fraud and abuse has grown exponentially as the size of government has grown over the past 60 years. For example, consider the problem that is often cited as that of the taking of improper payments.

According to the Brookings Institution, a nonprofit public policy organization, based in Washington, DC., the federal government issues tens of billions of dollars of payments each year to the wrong people or in the wrong amount or without the proper documentation. This is a real problem. Many of these payments are made to people who are dead or in jail and to companies that have actually been barred from doing business with the federal government. Then there's the waste and inefficiency from overlap and duplication within and across agencies. There are dozens of programs and offices throughout the federal government that are providing overlapping services to the same populations and they each incur their own administrative and program costs. It gets worst. I haven't even mentioned the billions upon billions that are wasted due to fraud or abuse that take place every day within all levels of government.

These are your taxpayer dollars we're talking about and all elected officials have a responsibility to spend your tax dollars wisely. Today more than ever we can no longer close our eyes to these issues. It is no longer acceptable today when we have a pressing need to rein in our spending and reduce our federal deficit. When families are watching every penny and making hard choices, they have a right to expect their government to do the same. All of this goes beyond waste. It results in missed opportunities to grow our economy, improve our education programs, and create more jobs. You deserve better from your government.

Getting Big Things Done in Government

When the government doesn't work as it should, it affects everything from whether small businesses can get loans, to whether students can get money for college, to whether our men and women in uniform can get the benefits they've earned. So when it comes to the organization and performance of our government, I think we can all agree that we're at a critical moment in our nation's history. The question is what are we going to do to do about it? Do we have the courage to do what it takes to build the government we need for the challenges we face. I ran for office because I believe we can.

I believe there are two steps to resolving the problems we have in government. First, we must rethink how our government is structured, how it works and how it is funded. Here we are 13 years into the 21st century, and states are still struggling with how to fund programs by using the 20th century methods for complex 21st century problems.

It seems to me that in many cases, these programs continue to exist simply because they existed the year before or because of the will of a small group of people. Where is the technology advancement? Where is the innovation in our government? From my point of view not much has changed in the past 50 years as to how government works.

New state leaders must embrace change, innovation, and new technology to address the problems of today. Everything must be open for debate and change. Every law, every regulation, every law passed by the Legislature can be repealed by the Legislature and that includes the creation of state agencies, burdensome regulations and fees that interfere with a free market. And, if the Legislature is unwilling to do this, then it's time we elect a Legislature that will. The second step requires the implementation of a proven, well documented method of management and operational excellence often referred to as Lean Six Sigma (LSS).

What Is Lean Six Sigma

Lean Six Sigma (LSS), according to George Washington University business professor Shivraj Kanungo, is "a set of tools, techniques, and a methodology that helps organizations improve their efficiency as well as their effectiveness." It is a blend of two corporate methodologies. "Lean" is a set of methods, initially developed by Toyota, used to ferret out waste, or non-value-added steps, in any repeatable process. This might tax collection, pot-hole filling, or delivering mail. "Six Sigma" developed by Motorola, is a set of methods that are used to reduce variation in any repeatable process. Together, the two methods eliminate waste and reduce variation in order to cut costs and improve quality.[44]

There are many organizations that use Lean Six Sigma to increase revenues, reduce costs, and improve collaboration. As you can see from the diagram there are a diverse range of industries including manufacturing, financial services, government, healthcare, and technology. You may wonder, "How can Lean Six Sigma be used in so many different organizations?" Well, the truth is that LSS is simply about solving problems efficiently and effectively.[45]

According to Michael George, Lean Six Sigma is a powerful, flexible and proven cost and waste elimination method that has been used successfully in both private and government organizations. As a business consultant, Mr. George created the Lean Six Sigma method for deep cost cuts, and through his firm the George Group, he brought his expertise at streamlining corporate processes to companies like Xerox and Caterpillar. Using his method, Motorola was able to return 1,500 manufacturing jobs to the U.S. which it had previously outsourced to China. Mike's Lean Six Sigma method was so successful at cutting waste in private enterprise that in 2004 the Department of

Defense hired the George Group to help tame runaway costs by training personnel in the process.[46]

Stunning Results

The Army reduced costs by approximately $22 billion in processes and programs to which it applied Lean Six Sigma. The Army Material Command alone is responsible for half of that savings by removing waste from the Army's supply chain. The Naval Warfare Systems Center in Charleston, SC achieved a tenfold increase in production of Mine Resistant Ambush Protected vehicles (used to protect soldiers from roadside bombs), with no new facilities and no additional employees. Another Navy facility achieved a fivefold increase in productivity and an 83 percent reduction in cycle time on aircraft engine repairs.[46]

Bringing the Efficiency of Private Enterprise to Government

Mr. George believed that there was no reason to accept continual increases in spending across the federal government without the kind of careful examination that has been successful with many military projects. He estimates that roughly 25 percent of all government spending is waste. Eliminating this waste across all federal agencies would slash between $500 and $700 billion dollars per year from the federal budget. That amount is roughly equal to the entire annual budget of the Department of Defense, and it is enough to start paying down the debt before the end of the decade.[46]

Let's apply this idea to state and local government. According to LSS exerts implementing LLS it would save Texas taxpayers $10-$15 billion each year and if the City of Corpus Christi would implement LLS it could save an estimated $50-$60 million per year. Imagine, how much LLS could save your local government.

Listed below are just a few of the many documented cases showing how effective and efficient the LSS process is.

Case Study of Ft. Wayne, Indiana

In the year 2000, the City of Ft. Wayne, Indiana was facing serious budget problems. All this changed when a new mayor, Graham Richard, was elected in 2000. Mr. Richard was an advocate of Lean Six Sigma even before he took office in 2000. During his eight years as mayor, he infected the city's employees with his enthusiasm. Even the city's nine unions joined the effort. In the ensuring years the city of Ft. Wayne, Indiana generated $30 million in savings for the city while at the same time improved the delivery of many city services. One notable improvement in services was the repairing of potholes.

Prior to the implementation of LLS, the city took 48 hours to repair one hole. After LLS was implemented it is now fixed within 3 hours of being reported. In addition to improving pothole repair, the city sewer treatment plant improved its operations. This was followed by the implementation of LLS in different departments resulting in the gradual change in the way the city did its work.

When Mayor Richard retired in January, 2008, the local newspaper, the News-Sentinel, editorialized about his term stating,

> "Mayor Richard has reduced crime to its lowest rate in over 20 years, kept taxes low and dramatically increased government efficiency with the implementation of Six Sigma, where millions of dollars have been saved and government jobs, such as filling potholes, have been reduced from 48 hours to three hours after the initial contact."[44]

Now this is change the American people can truly believe in!

LLS truly transformed the city from being a typical city with serious budget problems to an exceptional city with great service. LSS helped to reshape how employees viewed the public. Today, Ft. Wayne employees now see the citizens and businesses as customers, and focuses on maximizing the value delivered to those customers.[44] Mayor Graham Richard and the City of Fort Wayne are a great example of what can be accomplished when Lean Six Sigma methods are applied to government.

Case Study of Irving, Texas

In these difficult financial times it's important that governments at all levels make the best use of the money they have. This was the case with the City of Irving in 2006. The city of Irving, Texas hired a new city manager by the name of Tommy Gonzalez to help the city deal with this budget crisis. Mr. Gonzalez had prior knowledge of Lean Six Sigma that he acquired when he was serving in the U.S. Army.

The City of Irving's annual budget in 2006 was $189 million. He implemented LLS at a cost of $100,000 and within two years the results were amazing. The city budget had dropped to $168 million saving the city $20 million in two short years. In addition, the city was able to eliminate unnecessary steps in city operations, perform many services more quickly, departments began working together, and morale was higher among city employees. Since 2009 the City of Irving has saved $30 million because of the use of LLS in their city operations.

It is not just financial gains that have been witnessed. The City has also become much more efficient with their time. "The time it's given back to employees. We've eliminated 37,000 hours of wasted time for our employees, which really helps their morale as well as performance," said Mr. Gonzales.[47]

Other Case Studies

There are many other well documented cases where lean six sigma was implemented and a significant cost savings was obtained. Here are just a few:

Case Study	Result	Amount of Savings
U.S. Department of Defense—	Increased production from 5 vehicles/day to 50/day. Saved thousands of American lives	Priceless
Fort Wayne, Indiana	Improved city services	More than $10 million
Naval Air Systems Command	Completely eliminated unnecessary reporting	$360,000 per year
UCSF Medical Center Sterile Processing Dept.	Reduced costs, improved performance, saved lives	$1,000,000 per year
Environmental Protection Agency	Process eliminated large waste; reducing the cycle time 82%. Eliminated waste by 70%; cut up to another 13 months of cost.	Billions saved
U.S. Army-CC Army Depot	Decrease cost overruns by 73%	Billions saved

Bold Leadership Is Needed

Now you would think our elected leaders, especially in Texas, would sit up and take notice of this kind of news, but they don't. Why is that? Why do our elected representatives continue to ignore this simple, but powerful method to eliminate waste in government? Do they think that saving Texas taxpayers $30 million by using lean six sigma is just too little for them and not worth their time? Perhaps it's time you should tell your own government leaders of the accomplishments of the city of Fort Wayne, Indiana and Irving, Texas. Perhaps you need to tell them to implement Lean Six Sigma or you will elect someone else who will.

Beware Of The False Sense
Of Security Of Prosperity

During the past two years the White House has been telling us
that a solid economic recovery is taking place. It claims a slight
drop in unemployment from 9.1 percent in June 2011 to 7.6 percent
this year. Washington says that prices aren't going up as fast,
but they are still going up, and that the stock market is another
indication that our days of economic trouble are over. Meanwhile,
in May, 2013 the Texas Legislature approved the highest budget
in our state's history. According to the Texas Public Policy
Foundation, a conservative think tank based in Austin, the recently
adopted budget for FY 2014-2015 spent $22 billion more in total
funds than just two years ago.

Could it be that we have solved our financial problems once and
for all? Could it be that our elected leaders know something we
don't? Don't you believe them for one minute. I believe both
Washington and Austin are gambling with our children's future.
They are betting that this wave of recovery will last for many years.
Everyone in Texas knows that the primary driver behind our state's
economic boom is the increase activity in the Eagle Ford shale
area.

In the past two years, Texas' oil production has gone up 71 percent.
Texas is now home to one-fifth of all drilling rigs worldwide. The
Eagle Ford, which stretches 400 miles from Laredo northeast into
East Texas, is attracting more capital investment than any other oil
field on the planet. Yet, less than seven years ago the Eagle Ford
was little more than a blotch on a geology map.[48]

Nevertheless, I get this uneasy feeling about our Legislature'
growing dependence on all this prosperity. I am afraid that without
common sense restraints and limits on spending we will not be able
to meet our financial obligations in the near future. The numbers
just don't add up. Texas is experiencing the perfect storm: a
growing population, an increase in demand for services, a growing

debt problem, a very expensive pension program, and a temporary period of great prosperity. If we listen to history, she has many lessons to share with us.

One of the most glaring is that the world, a nation, a state will experience a period of financial prosperity that will be followed by a period of financial distress and hardship. History teaches us that history will repeat herself quiet often. Therefore, since we are in a period of financial prosperity it is only a matter of time that a period of financial distress will follow.

You see my friends, if you read the papers and all the press releases that come out of Austin they want us to think that all is well in Texas. Well, don't you believe them for one minute. The truth is that over the past 20 years during the time Texas was creating thousands of jobs and proclaiming that she was the model for all states, Texas government was also very busy in growing dramatically in size and in the amount of taxes it collects and spends. The truth is that in 2013 the Texas Legislature passed the largest spending budget in Texas history. In other words, Big Government is alive and well in Texas and this trend is not good for our state's economic future.

Everyone knows that as government grows bigger our liberty is diminished and we the people end up picking up the tab from the increase cost of more regulations, fees, taxes, and the increase cost of some government bureaucrat knocking on the door and saying to us, "I am from the government and I am here to help!" Once again, don't you believe them for one minute.

The Challenges Are Real

There is no doubt Texas is a state that has done a great job creating more jobs than the rest of America and this is something we all can be thankful for and proud of, but we also must acknowledge that Texas is confronted with many serious problems that need solving. These problems are not the result of any failure of the people; it is a failure of big government. It is big government that has gotten us where we are today.

For years politicians have talked about eliminating waste, fraud, and abuse. There is probably no other phase used more frequently in campaign speeches by politicians than this one. Nonetheless, state spending, continues to rise at a much faster level than what is economically essential and waste, fraud, and abuse continue to be present in large numbers.

FUTURE FINANCIAL NEEDS OF TEXAS

■ Local Debt	$321 billion
■ Transportation	315 billion
■ Water	231 billion
■ Education*	22 billion

* (86,000/year x $8,400 = $723 million/year x 30 years)

Total	**$889 billion**
$889/ 30 years	$29.6 billion/year

Other anticipated projected costs such as increases in Medicaid, pay raises, and cost of living are not included. Also, the amount used are the present value of cost as per the original report.

Today, I believe that almost every state in America, including Texas, is faced or will soon be faced with a pending financial crisis if they do not change how legislatures prepare the budget and control spending levels. Why? Simply because most state, county, and city governments are billions of dollars in debt, have pension plans they can no longer afford and continue to conduct business as usual with a decision making process and policies that will only make things worse with the passage of time, not better.

According to my estimates Texas is facing a $900 billion financial crisis in the next 15-30 years.[49] Imagine for a moment a car driving 90 miles an hour and the car is heading towards a cliff and the driver has no intention of changing directions. This is a picture of how the Texas Legislature has been handling the financial challenges facing the state of Texas.

The question our leaders must contend with is not if another financial crisis will come, but rather, when the next crisis will come. How will we handle the next great financial crisis when it hits us again could possibly determine Texas' economy for the ensuing 10 years? Will Texas handle it like it did in 2011 when Texas faced a $25 billion budget shortfall Texas chose to balance the budget without raising taxes or in 2003 when Texas was faced with a $10 billion shortfall and balanced that budget without raising taxes? I certainly hope so. In both previous cases, despite all the accusations by the liberal media and the Democrat Party that the world would come to an end and that people would be thrown out into the streets, the results that were achieved were nothing like it was projected, rather in both cases the economy of the state of Texas grew significantly.

The long-term answer to the unpredictable environment is in our ability to reduce the size of government, spend only what is absolutely necessary based on spending cap formula, and our ability to dramatically grow our economy. In other words, the achievements of the past 10 years will not pay for the challenges and opportunities we will face in the next 25 years.

We must not allow ourselves to be trapped into making a false choice of either making drastic cuts in spending or by raising revenues by increasing taxes or tapping into our state's emergency fund (saving account). There is another way.

That is why implementing Lean Six Sigma legislation into your local and state government, as we begin to do during the 2011 Texas legislative session, is so critically important. It provides us with a management tool we need to reduce waste and fraud in our state government that is conservatively projected to save Texas taxpayers $10-$15 billion per year. The implementation of Lean Six Sigma legislation is a bold step towards true government reform and the foundation for a new way of conducting state business designed to meet the complex problems we face in the 21st century.

"Nothing could be more obvious, nothing could be easier to solve—and yet politicians have done nothing. Strong America Now is here to change that because debt is our greatest threat."—Mike George

Our Challenges Represent Great Opportunities

"Failure is simply the opportunity to begin again, this time more intelligently."—Henry Ford

Someone once said, "With every challenge, there are great opportunities." Well, if that is true then we have more opportunities than what we know what to do with in Texas.

I have written, *Winning Now* because I wanted to be able to provide the answer to the many questions that concern citizens may have about their government. This book is a straight forward, common sense guide that can be used to guide you to transform your state government from being mediocre to being excellent. When we begin the journey I asked you to keep in mind there were lots of ways or reasons as to why your efforts can fail simply because there are many obstacles to accomplishing excellence in government.

Let me remind you that in order to succeed you must have a good cause or good idea that others are willing to support, a well written piece of legislation that explains the idea and how it works in government, the political support from a broad base of supporters preferably from both Republicans and Democrats, and a well written strategy for implementation.

Ultimately, every big step you take will be judged on the results it produces. Remember, In order to win, you must do so as a team. A team approach is critical to your success. The winners are those who understand how the process works, form a team of likeminded team members, and who are willing to work diligently to get their initiatives through long and often very difficult legislative process.

The possibility of failure is real and must be taken seriously. Therefore, prepare yourself to accept the reality that your desire to be successful may take many legislative sessions. This requires you to be very patient with others and with the process.

"Victory is won not in miles but in inches. Win a little now, hold your ground, and later, win a little more."—Louis L'Amour

Government will never voluntarily reduce itself, cut funding, or provide you and me with more freedoms. It is contrary to its nature. That is why we must fight this war over policy and ideas. States hold the key to our economic future. States always have, and always will compete for residents, revenues, and industries. Competition is the foundation of success and economic strength in this country. The stronger our states are individually, the stronger our nation is as a whole. As states continue to sort out budgets and finances, Texas is certainly the example to follow. No matter which state you're in, by letting people keep more of their money, limiting government interference, and maintaining fiscal discipline, your state can create an environment that fosters opportunity and prosperity for its citizens, while expanding the engine for America's renewed economic growth.

Despite the economic difficulties facing all the states, there is a way to transform your state government. I believe that if you implement the proven legislative policies and general ideas found in this book and in many other books, you can assist your elected officials to make informed decisions and build solid ideas that have been proven to work anywhere in the world. After all that is what *Winning Now* is all about.

"In Texas, we've worked hard to foster an environment that frees employers to do what they do best—dream big, meet challenges and create jobs, and employers of all sizes and from all industries are discovering the Texas advantage and bringing jobs with them,"—Rick Perry

Achieving Excellence In Government

"The failure of national economic policy is costing us more than jobs; it has begun to weaken that uniquely American spirit of risk-taking, large ambition, and optimism about the future. We must rally them now to bold departures that rebuild our national morale as well as our material prosperity."—Mitch Daniels

The history of the United States of America is can be defined as a history of individual achievement. It was our ancestor's hard work that built our many cities and farmed millions of acres of farmland. It was their steadfast determination and intellect that lead them to continually push beyond the boundaries of the impossible. They reshaped our world with the steam engine, telephone, light bulb, automobile, polio vaccine, desktop computer and smartphone. It was their love of freedom and faith in country that sustained them through trials, hardships and through wars, and it was their courage and self-sacrifice that enabled them to always prevail.

If Texas is to lead in the 21st Century we need this kind of American spirit and achievement. Let me begin by saying we have, in our lifetime, done more to feed the poor, heal the sick, and liberate those living in tyranny than any people who ever lived on this earth. Yet, despite all this good, we in America are struggling to get by. Our families are hurting and the gap between the rich and the middle class is getting wider by the day. The people want answers to our problems.

Big Government Is The Problem

It is for this reason why seeking to reform our government is so critical to the future of our state and our nation. States like Texas must learn from the mistakes of states like California, who has for years increased its public debt and spent all the money that flows into the state treasury. These are the practices that have gotten them on the brink of bankruptcy. If Texas and other states continue to increase its public debt and continues to spend all the money in the Treasury it will not be long before states find ourselves in the same dilemma as California.

Big government is alive and well in Texas and all over America. Some of you may not know this but in the last four years the Texas Legislature has passed over 3,000 new laws. I thought our so called "conservative" leadership and Texas Legislators were supposed to represent us and protect from a runaway government? From the looks of things that doesn't seem to be the case.

I wish to offer the Texas Legislature and other state legislatures a simple and genuine idea. Instead of passing a thousand new laws the next time the Legislature meets why don't they try eliminating a few hundred of them? The people would vote for that in a heartbeat. In addition, over the past three legislative sessions the Legislature has managed to approve an increase in fees and government regulations. What was the net result of all this change in government? The truth is we the people now have the dubious honor and privilege to pay more for everything we buy such as food, gas, and typical household items.

How much bigger is government today than 20 years ago? How about a lot bigger!

Just took around and it will not take you long to see that every conceivable kind of job in our economy requires some kind of government license, permit, or certification. From serving food at a restaurant, or fixing a water leak in our homes government now has found a way to tax just about everything that moves.

We Must Rethink The Role Of Government

Let me be clear, we're not going to have real prosperity in the long run until we stop fighting the symptoms and start fighting the disease. The disease is the enormous growth of government. There's only one cure for this and that is a zero based budget and a Constitutional provision to limit the growth of state spending to population growth plus inflation, the growth in personal income, or the growth in gross state product, whichever is less. Yet, our legislators have not even taken a vote on these two simple, but powerful ideas during the past four sessions.

If you ask the career politicians why we don't take bold steps to reign in the size government many of them will say that it is too hard and time consuming for legislators and budget administrators to do use zero base budgeting and that 85 percent or so of the spending in the budget is fixed by laws passed by the Texas Legislature. Well, I have a simple answer to these problems. Laws passed by the Legislature can be repealed by the Legislature and that includes the creation of state agencies, burdensome regulations and fees that interfere with a free market. And, if the Legislature is unwilling to do this, then isn't it time we elect a Legislature that will?

Here is another problem I see in Austin. Earlier this year Governor Perry asked the Legislature to include in the new budget a $1.6 billion tax cut as part of the new budget. Well, my question then is, "If there is room for a $1.6 billion tax cut, what was it doing there in the first place?"

Unfortunately, Austin legislators and bureaucrats don't feel the same pain from high taxes and fees that you and I do. As a matter of fact, government makes a profit on every dollar of sales tax, property tax, or excise tax that is collected every day and it seems they are set on collecting even more taxes. That is not the role of government.

It would have been nice if our legislators would decide to reduce the size of government so they don't have to raise more taxes to feed the government's hunger. But, I get this uncomfortable feeling that our state government has adopted the same principles of the feral government that says, "If it moves tax it."

I believe that if government is operated like we operate our homes and our businesses then government could solve many of the problems facing us today. I am convinced that career politicians, those who have been part of the problem, are not necessarily the best qualified to solve those problems. Albert Einstein once said, ""We cannot solve our problems with the same level of thinking that created them." How true this is.

I believe we can solve any problem quickly and without raising new taxes if and only if we take the politics out of the equation and use some much needed common sense. You see I believe God had a divine purpose when he created this great land we call America. He did it so that those people who had a hunger for freedom and the courage to leave their homeland only to face unknown dangers just so they could have the opportunity to be free men.

From our forefathers to our modern-day immigrants, we've come from every corner of the earth only to be called Americans. On the campaign trail I see people from all walks of life busy at work, getting an education, or starting a new business all in the hopes that one day their dreams will come true and they do so despite the interferences and hardships placed upon them by the federal government.

Today, big government is our master. Just like slaves were treated over hundred years ago, today's career politicians and government officials would have us believe that we are incapable of managing our own lives. Our government has grown in its practice of governing in secret. The Austin elites tell us it's too complex for our understanding.

Perhaps that is why the state's budget is so hard to read and understand. Perhaps that is why so many cities, counties, and school districts refuse to post their budgets on line for all the world to see. Why else would they act this way? Could it be that they truly believe that we might panic if we were to be told the truth? Could it be that if we found out they got us into these problems that just maybe, we would get mad and fire them? It makes me wonder.

I have a question for them? Why should we become frightened? History has shown us that there isn't any problem that "We the People" can't solve if government would just give us the facts, all the facts. Then, get out of the way and let us have at it.

I am convinced there is more common sense at a high school PTA meeting or at a farmer's Co-Op meeting than in all the combine brain power found in government bureaucrats or career politicians. I am convinced that the private sector can solve all of our biggest problems if only the Austin elites would invite them to do that.

I want to believe that one day soon we will have better government. I believe our nation hungers for a spiritual revival; hunger to see once again see our elected leaders do what is right in the eyes of the people; hunger to see our elected leaders listen to us; and to see government once again be the protector of our liberties, not the supplier of gifts to the privilege. I believe government should honor and protect those institutions which support and protect the very values upon which our civilization is founded—God, life and family.

If Texas is to prosper for many years to come and if Texas is to continue leading America in individual and economic freedom we must return government back to what she was meant to be. But, in order to do this we need elected leaders who are independent of the forces that have brought us our problems—the Congress, Legislature, the bureaucracy, the lobbyist, and big labor.

If we are to survive and prosper, government must change, made limited, sooner than later. However, it will only change when "We the people" vote for a leadership that listens to us, relies on us and seeks to return government to us. We need a government that is confident not of what it can do, but of what the people can do.

Looking forward I believe it is vital that we continue to talk in plain English about responsible, responsive, and measurable government. I firmly believe that we the people should decide how much government we want, not some politician or special interest group. I don't believe for one moment that four more years of business-as-usual in Austin and Washington is the answer to our problems, and I don't think the American people believe it either.

Only time will tell us what America and Texas will look like 20 years from now. Still I wonder what kinds of questions our grandchildren will ask us 20 years from now. Perhaps the questions they ask will be, "Grandpa, what was America like when you were growing up?" Or perhaps, "Grandpa, what did you do 20 years ago to keep America free?" Well, I hope none of us will not have to tell them, "I didn't do anything. I was too afraid to try."

I firmly believe the majority of Americans are not happy if we are not moving forward. Everywhere I have traveled I hear over and over again that Americans want a country that is growing and thriving once again. A country that is able to solve its problems with a government they can trust and that promotes and protects the productive workers more rather than the unproductive; a government that tells us the truth instead of making empty promises; a government that gives us hope and faith instead of excuses and despair.

When these things happen then, the people will be renewed, their confidence restored and then I believe America will release that energy that is the most powerful force in the world, the American spirit. That is the America that once was our home. That is the America millions seek once again. And that is how we can build a better Texas Tomorrow beginning today.

In closing let us remember the words of Hall of Fame Coach Vince Lombardi who said, "Perfection is not attainable, but if we chase perfection, we can catch excellence." This sums up what *Winning Now* is about. *Winning Now* provides us with a strategy and a pathway, which if followed, can and will transform your state government from being ordinary to achieving excellence in your state government.

What remains to be seen is what you choose to do. The truth is that your children and your grandchildren will know the end result of your efforts.

"Life is a gift, and it offers us the privilege, opportunity, and responsibility to give something back by becoming more."—Tony Robbins

About the Author

Raul Torres, is the author of *Texas Tomorrow: An Economic Plan for Texas in the 21st Century.* Raul Torres served in the Texas House of Representatives from 2011 through 2013 where he represented District 33 in Corpus Christi.

Raul is a licensed Certified Public Accountant and has owned and operated Raul Torres, CPA, a full service accounting and financial services firm, since 1993. He graduated from Corpus Christi State University with a Bachelor of Business Administration with a major in Accounting and a minor in Finance. He obtained a Masters of Business Administration degree from Texas A&M University-Corpus Christi in 1994.

In addition to being a licensed CPA, he is also a President of Freedom Tax Services, Inc, a Liberty Tax Service franchisee, and owner of Raul Torres Insurance Agency. He is a member of the Texas Society of Certified Public Accountants and the International Association of Registered Financial Consultants, Inc.

While in the Texas House of Representatives, Raul served on the Appropriations and Insurance Committees. He authored key legislation, SB 563, which was designed to eliminate wasteful government spending. He also carried legislation to bring additional economic development and jobs to the city of Corpus Christi. He also carried legislation returning approximately $77 million from the state to cities and counties, resulting in his being honored with Texas Municipal League's Legislator of the Year Award for 2011. He also earned the Texas Association of Benefit Administrator's "Top Ten Legislator" Award, the Texas Association of Business "Fighter of Free Enterprise" Award for his support of the business community and the "Defender of the American Dream" Award from Americans for Prosperity—Texas.

Raul is active in community service. He previously served on the Loan Review Board and the Traffic Advisory Board for the City of Corpus Christi. Raul has been involved and has supported local youth sports programs and band booster clubs. Raul and his wife Gina are proud parents of five children and seven grandchildren and are members of the Church of Christ.

"For God so loved the world that he gave his one and only Son, that whoever believes in him shall not perish but have eternal life."—Jesus Christ

Endnotes

[1] Rowen, Beth. (2013) *History of the Tea Party Movement.* http://www.infoplease.com/us/government/tea-party-history.html [accessed 10/31/2013].

[2] Texas Legislative Council. (2010). *How A Bill Becomes A Law.* http://www.house.state.tx.us/about-us/bill/ [accessed 6/15/2013]

[3] Texas Legislative Council. (2010). *Process for a Bill.* http://www.house.state.tx.us/about-us/bill/ [accessed 6/15/2013]

[4] Reilly, Mollie. (2013) *Congress Disapproval Rating Hits All-Time High In NBC/WSJ Poll, Obama Approval Drops.* http://www.huffingtonpost.com/2013/07/24/congress-disapproval-rating_n_3642480.htm [accessed 6/15/2013]

[5] Lutz, Dr. Frank (2011) *Win*, New York: Hyperion Publishing

[6] Galston William. (2011) *Rebuilding Public Trust in Government: Where We've Been, Where We Are, Where We Need to Go.* http://www.thedemocraticstrategist.org/strategist/2011/03/rebuilding_public_trust_in_gov.php [accessed 6/15/2013]

[7] Pew Center on the States and the Public Policy Institute of California. (2010) *Facing Facts: Public Attitudes and Fiscal Realities in Five Stressed States.* http://heartland.org/sites/all/modules/custom/heartland_migration/files/pdfs/28560.pdf [accessed 6/15/2013]

[8] McCann, Bailey. (2011) *Michigan communities join other cities, states in banning electronic communication during public meetings.* http://www.govloop.com/profiles/blogs/michigan-communities-join [accessed 6/15/2013]

[9] *Schwartz, David McGrath. (2011), Governor signs health care transparency bills into law.* http://www.lasvegassun.com/news/2011/jun/24/governor-signs-health-care-transparency-bills-law/ [accessed 6/15/2013]

[10] CivSource. (2010) *Virginia starts streaming transportation meetings online.* http://civsourceonline.com/2010/05/11/virginia-starts-streaming-transportation-meetings-online/ [accessed 6/15/2013]

[11] Noveck, Beth Simone (2009) *Wiki Government: How Technology Can Make Government Better, Democracy Stronger, and Citizens More Powerful.* Washington, DC: Brookings Institution Press.

[12] Gilroy Leonard and Jonathan Williams. (2011) *State Budget Reform Toolkit,* Washington D.C: American Legislative Exchange Council

[13] Segal, Geoffrey. (2005) *Virginia Spending and Budget Reform.* Springfield: Thomas Jefferson Institute for Public Policy

[14] Pew Center On The States. (2011) *The Widening Gap: The great recession's impact on state pension and retiree health care cost.* Washington D.C.: The Pew Charitable Trusts.

[15] Poulson, Dr. Barry W. and Dr. Arthur P. Hall. (2010) *State Pension Funds Fall Off a Cliff.* Washington D.C.: American Legislative Exchange Council

[16] Quintero, James. (2012) *On the Comptroller's New Public Pension Report.* Austin: Texas Public Policy Foundation.

[17] Luhby, Tami. (2011) *N.J. governor wants workers to pay more for benefits.* http://money.cnn.com/2011/02/22/news/economy/

New_Jersey_budget_Chris_christie/index.htm [accessed 8/10/2013]

[18] Wall Street Journal. (2011) *The Utah Pension Model.* http://online.wsj.com/news/articles/SB1000142405274870358340457608 0260001386474 [accessed 8/10/2013]

[19] Young, Elizabeth. (2010) *Testimony to the Senate State Affairs Committee.* Austin: Texas Public Policy Foundation.

[20] Davidson John. (2013) *Three Proactive Health Insurance Reforms for Texas.* Austin: Texas Public Policy Foundation.

[21] Wohlgemuth, Arlene & Spencer Harris. (2011) *The Big Squeeze.* Austin: Texas Public Policy Foundation.

[22] Wohlgemuth, Arlene Brittani Miller and Spencer Harris. (2011) *Medicaid Reform: Constructive Alternatives to a Failed Program.* Austin: Texas Public Policy Foundation.

[23] Peacock, Bill. (2011) *Texas' Economic Leadership Due to Our Leadership in Limited Government Policies. Austin*: Texas Public Policy Foundation.

[24] Lindley Kevin. (2011) *Gov. Perry Announces eBay to Create More Than 1,000 High-Paying Jobs in Austin.* http://www.rickperry.org/blog/gov-perry-announces-ebay-create-more-1000-high-paying-jobs-austin [accessed 8/19/2013]

[25] Office of Governor Rick Perry. (2013) *Texas Emerging Technology Fund.* http://www.texaswideopenforbusiness.com/incentives-financing/tetf.php [accessed 8/19/2013]

[26] Liebelson, Dana. (2013) *Rick Perry's $487 Million Corporate Slush Fund Doesn't Need Your Stinkin' Audit.* http://www.motherjones.com/politics/2013/03/rick-perry-texas-enterprise-fund-audit [accessed 12/18/2013]

[27] Cohn, Scott. (2012) *Texas Is America's Top State for Business 2012.* http://www.cnbc.com/id/47818860 [accessed 12/21/2013]

[28] Laffer, Arthur, Donna Arduin, and Stephen Moore. (2010) *Competitive States 2010: Texas vs. California.* Austin: Texas Public Policy Foundation

[29] Annenberg Public Policy Center. (2011) *Texas-Size Recovery.* Annenberg Public Policy Center. http://www.factcheck. org/2011/08/texas-size-recovery/ [accessed 12/21/2013]

[30] Laffer, Arthur. (2008) *Entrepreneurs versus Regulators: Government Intervention in the Market.* Austin: Texas Public Policy Foundation.

[31] Garfield, Reed. (2012) *Smothering economic growth one regulation at a time.* http://tribes.tribe.net/america/thread/d288e1c7-9142-4990-85f3-2ea1f84a872c [accessed 8/21/2013]

[32] Crews Jr., Clyde Wayne. (2013) *Ten Thousand Commandments: An Annual Snapshot of the Federal Regulatory State.* Washington D.C.: Competitive Enterprise Institute.

[33] Adelmann, Bob. (2013) *Cost Estimate of Government Regulations Doesn't Measure the Real Cost.* http://www.thenewamerican.com/ usnews/congress/item/15458-cost-estimate-of-government-regulations-doesn-t-measure-the-real-cost [accessed 12/21/2013]

[34] Young, Ryan and Wayne Crews. (2012) *Washington's Ten Thousand Commandments.* http://spectator.org/archives/2012/06/05/ washingtons-ten-thousand-comma [accessed 9/18/2013]

[35] Hahn, Robert W. and Robert E. Litan. (1997) *Improving Regulatory Accountability.* Washington, D.C.: American Enterprise Institute for Public Policy Research and the Brookings Institution.

[36] Torres, Justin. (2011) *Case Study: Texas Tort Reform.* http://www.tortreform.com/news/case-study-texas-tort-reform [accessed 9/25/2013]

[37] Texans for Lawsuit Reform. (2008) *The Impact of Lawsuit Reform on economic activity in the Lone Star state.* http://www.tlrfoundation.com/perryman-group-report [accessed 9/27/2013]

[38] Cauchon, Dennis. (2011) *Texas wins in U.S. economy shift*, USA Today, June 21, 2011. http://usatoday30.usatoday.com/money/economy/2011-06-20-state-gdp-growth_n.htm [accessed 10/2/2013]

[39] U.S. Department of Labor (2013) Texas Employment Statistics. http://data.bls.gov/timeseries/LASST48000005?data_tool=XGtable [accessed 12/22/2013]

[40] Laffer, Dr. Arthur B. Laffer, Stephen Moore, and Jonathan Williams. (2013) *Rich States, Poor States 6th Edition.* Washington D.C.: American Legislative Exchange Council.

[41] Steinhauser Paul. (2010) *CNN Poll: Majority think government is broken.* http://politicalticker.blogs.cnn.com/2010/02/21/cnn-poll-majority-think-government-is-broken/ [accessed 10/2/2013]

[42] Edggers, William, Robert Campbell III, and Tiffany D. Fishman. (2010). *Letting Go of the Status Quo—A Playbook for Transforming State Government.* Winnipeg: Deloitte Public Leadership Institute.

[43] Eggers, William D., Robert Wavra, Lisa Snell, and Adrian Moore. (2005) *Driving More Money into the Classroom: The Promise of Shared Services.* Washington D.C.: Reason Foundation.

[44] Kamensky, John M. (2008) *Is Lean Six Sigma "Cool? Ask Employees of Ft. Wayne, Indiana!" IBM Center for The Business of Government.* http://www.businessofgovernment.org/brief/lean-six-sigma-cool-ask-employees-ft-wayne-indiana [accessed 10/12/2013]

45 GoLeanSixSigma.com (2013) *Lean Six Sigma Simplified: What Is Lean Six Sigma.* http://www.goleansixsigma.com/lean-six-sigma-simplified/webinar/what-is-lean-six-sigma.html [accessed 12/19/2013]

46 Gingrich, Newt. (2011) *Mike George Wants to Save You $500 Billion a Year and Balance the Budget by 2017.* http://www.humanevents.com/2011/06/29/mike-george-wants-to-save-you-500-billion-a-year-and-balance-the-budget-by-2017/ [accessed 10/12/2013]

47 Gaskell, Adi. (2012) *Texas City Saves $30 million by Using Lean Six Sigma.* http://technorati.com/politics/article/texas-city-saves-30-million-by

48 Wilder, Forrest. (2013) *The Oil Boom is Back, but at What Cost?* http://www.texasobserver.org/the-oil-boom-is-back-but-at-what-cost/ [accessed 12/22/2013]

49 Torres, Raul. (2013) *Texas Tomorrow: The Future of Texas.* http://www.slideshare.net/rtcpa2000/texas-tomorrow-the-future-of-texas-by-raul-torres-cpa [accessed 12/22/2013]